Re-Authoring the World

Dearest Emily

Many blessings in re-authoring
all the narratives that matter
to you deeply!

Much love

Re-Authoring the World

The Narrative Lens and Practices for Organisations, Communities and Individuals

Chené Swart

KNOWRES
PUBLISHING

2013

First published in 2013

ISBN: 978-1-86922-427-1

Published by Knowres Publishing (Pty) Ltd
P O Box 3954
Randburg
2125
Republic of South Africa

Tel: (011) 706-6009
Fax: (011) 706 1127
E-mail: orders@knowres.co.za
Website: www.kr.co.za

Printed and bound: Mega Digital (Pty) Ltd, Parow Industria, Cape Town
Typesetting, layout and design: Cia Joubert, cia@knowres.co.za
Cover design: Nadia du Plessis, nadia@designfigment.co.za
Illustrations: Lana Oosthuizen, lanaoosthuizen@gmail.com
Photo: Harriet Kaufman
Editing and proofreading: Elsa Crous, getitedited@mweb.co.za
Project management: Cia Joubert, cia@knowres.co.za
Index created with: TExtract, www.Texyz.com

To Beloved Friends
Manna at the table of companionship
-See you soon-

CONTENTS

ACKNOWLEDGEMENTS

In my first class at the Institute for Therapeutic Development in Pretoria in 2002, Dr Elmarie Kotzé introduced herself by sharing with us the stories of gratitude she has for a community of people on whose shoulders she stands.[1] As my feet are planted on the African continent, with its deeply rooted communal understanding of identity, it is a privilege for me now to honour the shoulders I am standing on. These 'shoulders' have not only supported the writing of this book, but have been collaborators, co-constructers and co-writers.

In Narrative work we are aware that we cannot but see the world through our own culture, nation and worldview or paradigm. Given the emphasis on our narratives in this work, we know that people are not objective clean slates as they enter any conversation. They are informed by a multiplicity of narratives, cultures, gifts, values, hopes, dreams and possibilities. In writing this book, I know that I was also informed by the multiplicities of my world and life. The particularities of my local tradition, community, culture, neighbourhood and context are rich gifts that inform the descriptions of the alternative narrative I am living in this world.

Africa

I stand on the shoulders of and am informed by the African continent, that has taught me change is the only constant, that there is a dance for every occasion, that there is a spiritual world beyond what we call reality, and that greeting and truly seeing one another are crucial to the experience of humanity.

South Africa

I am informed by the South African history of pain and possibility. I have tasted the fear of a nation in transition, and I am now celebrating the rich and diverse tapestry of alternative narratives arising every day. Our history has forced us to be the answer to the alternative, and within all our challenges and problem stories, the exceptions are always present. We bring to the world the gift of reconciliation, open and honest conversations around our differences, and stories of how these conversations influence us. We dare to talk openly about what matters.

Afrikaner

In addition, I see the world through the eyes of my Afrikaner culture with its pioneering spirit, a willingness to explore the world, the belief that we can always make a plan, and a strong belief in God. I also come from the dark history of the Afrikaners' implementation and institutionalisation of apartheid in South Africa. This painful history privileged me because I benefited from the various

---

1   Elmarie Kotzé is a lecturer in Narrative therapy at the University of Waikato in Hamilton, New Zealand. Elmarie and Dirk Kotzé started the Institute for Therapeutic Development that ran Master's and doctoral programmes in practical theology, specialising in pastoral therapy, with the University of South Africa in Pretoria.

possibilities that were available, while the voices of black, Indian and coloured people were silenced and discriminated against. I stand on the shoulders of all the black women who have helped and supported me so that I could write and learn.

OD and HR communities

Organisational Development (OD) and Human Resource (HR) communities in South Africa have been at the forefront of co-constructing new ways of being in the business world since our first democratic election in 1994. They have imagined and co-journeyed with work-communities in transformational processes that facilitate crucial conversations to take us forward. I stand on the shoulders of a gracious, patient and visionary OD and HR community in South Africa which has taught me the language of their work and invited me to bring the Narrative ideas to this field.

Work-communities

As a consultant and coach I have worked in the corporate and community fields, applying Narrative ideas in various contexts. Therefore, every individual, team, community and organisation is a participant, a co-writer and co-author of this book, as we learned together over the past eight years. This book exists because I stand on the shoulders of clients who dared to re-author their narratives on an individual, team, communal and organisational level.

Mining community

For several years I had the privilege of being on a journey with some of the major platinum mining houses in South Africa, and I especially acknowledge the important influence this unique work community has had on what and how I am able to write and see.

These mining communities have made me aware that even though we might smile and seem to get along despite our differences, our stories are a crucial connector and an opening for the conversation of the gift of difference that we bring.

I have been taught in various workshops by participants about how important it is to invite all the knowledges in the room to participate in a conversation; about how facilitators need to deconstruct their power and the language they use to open up a conversation rather than shut it down. We still have people in these workshops who cannot read and write. Including everybody's voice through our life stories makes us all equal in our humanness.

I see the world through different languages. Even as I write, I am doing it in my second language. For most of the time, workshop participants in the mining context are conversing in their second language (and sometimes even their third language). Inviting participants to speak and express themselves in their first language allows one to mine rich stories, metaphors and images that we can all learn from. From the miner underground, to the office worker above ground – there is a multiplicity of narratives which are treasures in themselves.

Religious communities

I have been raised in religious communities and have seen the dark and light side of the potential such communities can bring. Just as we have our cultural and language differences in South Africa, so too the rich tapestry of religious differences expands the diverse stories of our country even more.

Neighbourhood

I see my country and my work from the beautiful neighbourhood where I live. It is a neighbourhood where I feel absolutely safe and cared for, with 24-hour surveillance as neighbours take turns to patrol, be available for any counselling, and phone me when they are concerned about me. In chapter eight I will say more about the alternative story of the neighbourhood that I am privileged to live in.

Colleagues, collaborators and community of concern

I stand on the shoulders of my friend Peter Block, who was the first to encourage me to write. His interest in the work, his questions and ideas have helped me to become clearer about my thoughts, to pay attention as I do the work, and to start imagining a world and a future beyond individual transformation.

I also stand on the shoulders of the ideas, questions, challenges, prophetic voices and imagination of Walter Brueggemann and Olivia Saunders.

I want to thank all the narrative practitioners in South Africa and across the world who have taught me and opened this lens to my life and work. A special word of thanks goes to Stephen Madigan, who gave me the opportunity to speak and present my work at the Narrative Therapeutic Conversations X in Vancouver in 2012. Stephen also introduced me to Pierre Blanc-Sahnoun, who is now a great colleague and friend of mine in the work of Narrative Organisational Practices.

A community of concern not only imagined the possibility of this book with me, but journeyed with me as I re-authored my own life narrative.[2] Special gratitude goes to Gayle, Joan, Darryl, Charles, Angeles, Ward, Kranti, A Small Group in Cincinnati, Carl, Francois, Karien, Johan, Sarah, Theo, Henja, Jan-Harm, Pieter, Lungie, Matumelo, Mwai, Thandi, Lerato and all the participants of the Narrative workshops that I have presented.

I am grateful to Leslie Stephen for editing the text with such respect and care, really coming alongside me in expressing the work and its intentions in a clear and poetic manner. Many thanks also go to Heidi Moore, Ben Kaufmann and numerous

---

2   Madigan, S & Epston, D 1998. *From 'Spy-chiatric Gaze' to Community of Concern*. David Epston and Stephen Madigan use the term "community of concern" in the context of a group of people who have been journeying with similar problem stories and become a community whose members spy together on the tactics of the problem and provide a community of support to one another. When I use this term, it describes a community that the participant has chosen to stand with him/her and to support him/her in exploring and living an alternative story. Alice Morgan (*What is Narrative Therapy?* p. 77) refers to this group or community of people as Life Club Members.

others who read the first draft and gave their insights, asked questions and helped to shape the text in a profound way. Our collective effort has contributed to the richness of the flavour of the book like a good red wine.

I am glad to thank all my family members who have been shoulders of care and prayer in this journey of writing. A special thanks to Nico, Jandro, Berno and my parents, Attie and Joanie.

Transformative work

In my journeys with colleagues and clients, friends and family, I witness transformation every day. As a result, I am given a platform to speak, participate and be transformed again and again. The Narrative work speaks of the intersection of the individual and communal narrative that is held in interdependence. This provides a richness and accessibility to transformation as an outcome of the work.

The Narrative work has bestowed so many gifts on me over the past years – gifts of transformation that again spill over into the transformation of groups and teams. We have celebrated the curiosity in the room. We have openly shared our narratives with vulnerability and acknowledged the expertise of the storytellers we have been privileged to listen to. We have opened up to strangers. We have discovered the possibility offered by the alternative path. We have accepted the freedom of choice and acknowledged how naming can give and take away power. We have experienced that we are not alone, and discovered how connected we are. We have celebrated how many gifts we received in community. We saw pieces of our own stories in others. We have named the status quo and questioned it. We have appreciated that our stories are important, even though they seemed less significant than others' stories. We have realised that we do not have to fix ourselves or one another. We have come to accept ourselves and feel supported by others in our transitions. We have acknowledged that we have the freedom to re-write our stories.

My dedication to the Narrative work helps me gain clarity about where and what kind of problem stories I want to re-write and participate in. My alternative narrative lives into reconciliation and is also the means of reconciliation. This reconciliation does not only come from me as an Afrikaner, but is constructed between workers and management in opening up a space for management where listening and being connected is the action step.

I am filled with so much gratitude for all the collaborators of this alternative narrative of transformation and voice in the working community and the new South Africa. I am no longer unwritten, but co-written. I have the fingerprints of the above communities upon whom I stand, all over my life and writing. To this work of transformation I am giving my life and heart. Being a collaborator in the re-authoring of our world is how I want to spend my life.

WELCOME

I started writing this book when my friend, Peter Block, invited me to explain the Narrative approach to him. It grew from my response to his initial request for the ten key elements of the Narrative work through several conversations and drafts into the book you now hold.

This book was also written to respond to Narrative workshop participants, Organisational Development (OD) and Human Resource (HR) consultants, coaches, leaders and managers who often asked me, "So what can I read?" The available literature in Narrative therapy is primarily focused on the therapeutic world and often does not address the needs and curiosities of the individuals and communities I journey with. The subtitle of this book therefore acknowledges organisations, communities and individuals outside of the therapeutic field as the audience I am writing this book for.

With this book I would like to support people who are interested in applying Narrative ideas beyond the edges of the therapeutic context in their work with individuals, teams, communities and organisations, as part of **re-authoring**[3] the fields of coaching, consulting, leadership, community engagement, teambuilding, debriefing, conflict management and diversity work. I am writing to all the HR and OD practitioners who have been my teachers of the language and world in which they serve. So many people have enabled me to bring the Narrative ideas to **work-communities** in different sectors, daring to talk and be in transformational ways in a world overwhelmed and dominated by the stories of business.[4]

I am also writing to the leaders and managers who want to be part of the re-authoring and re-writing of their own stories, the stories of work-communities and all other forms of communities in this world. In addition to the interest the corporate world has exhibited in Narrative ideas, I started to receive invitations to be part of conversations that have in mind the shift from **problem narratives** to **alternative narrative**s in other fields – particularly the arts, economics, community work, education, religion and womanhood. I was even invited into a conversation around the shifting of a nation's story.

This book is an invitation to learn and apply practices that enable individuals, teams, families, communities, organisations and nations to co-create alternative narratives by taking back the pen to the storytelling rights of their lives and worlds. This book is also written for everyone who believes that a different narrative about self, neighbour, communities, nations, economics, arts, education and religion (and this is not a comprehensive list) is possible and wants to explore practices and methodologies that are vehicles for transformation in shifting narratives that no longer serve us.

---

3   When first introduced, certain terms that appear in the glossary are printed in bold type to draw the reader's attention to them and to signal that the definition is captured in the glossary, for convenient memory-refreshing later on.

4   Pierre Blanc-Sahnoun introduced me to the idea of speaking about the workforce as work-communities, which opens up much richer descriptions and possibilities. I use the terms "work-communities" and "community of workers" interchangeably.

This book is for all who cannot sit back in a state of docility claiming that what we have is just the way things are. The ideas in this book are based on the belief that our participation in the world really matters, and that collective ownership of our world can move us forward into an alternative narrative towards the common good.[5] I am writing to all who are willing to participate in the transformation of our world, one narrative at a time.

A warning: If you believe that the way things are in this world is good and acceptable, and will create a future you can live with, then this book is not for you. If you are looking for nice new ideas to add to your toolbox for working with individuals and communities, then this book is not for you. The ideas birthed from the Narrative approach are not a collection of 'nice' techniques and methodologies that can be divorced from the philosophical ground and values of the work.

ORIGINS AND DESTINATIONS

The ideas, reflections and representations of the Narrative practices explored and discussed in this book flow from all my conversations with practitioners, friends and workshop participants. They are my own interpretations and applications of the ideas and in no way represent the voices of all who work with Narrative ideas. My intentions with the book are to provide a survey of the territory and to inspire readers to explore the applications of Narrative ideas and practices within their organisational, community and family lives.

I structured the book to provide different portals into understanding, and you can roam about in the chapters you are interested in. If you do not want to read the whole book, you can read short descriptions of the different parts at the start of each section:

Part one provides the background and context. It tells the story of how the Narrative ideas transform and inform one's life and work, starting with one of my own stories.

Part two is my description of the theory and concepts. It describes and unpacks the values and assumptions that inform the Narrative work.

Part three explores the practices and processes of the Narrative work.

Part four shows how the Narrative work is applied in coaching, leadership and consulting.

Part five delves into the transformational nature of the Narrative work.

The Introduction offers a broad overview of the origins and intentions of the Narrative approach and provides a glimpse into the possibilities the Narrative lens brings into focus. The first chapter of the book begins with how the Narrative work has influenced my own life, and opens up the ideas and approach through

---

5   Brueggemann, W 2010. *Journey to the Common Good.*

one of my own life stories. This is an ethical choice, as what I am able to write and see in this world is hugely influenced by the multiplicity of my own life stories, community, culture and country. I do not write objectively, meaning that I cannot be in a state where I am untouched by these things. Starting the book with one of my own stories invites you into the stories that inform this book, and also explains the Narrative ideas by referring to this chosen story.

Taken as whole, this book makes the Narrative approach and practices a lens and a set of tools with which to see and participate in individual, communal and organisational stories. It provides you, the reader, with my interpretation and understanding of the heart of the work, the skills to practise the work, and a way to see yourself and your place in the world. You will be invited to talk and listen in transformational ways. This book will open up the possibility of creating spaces where the human and the communal narrative can be transformed.

INTRODUCTION TO THE NARRATIVE APPROACH

The Narrative approach was founded on and grew from the construction of respectful practices with people in counselling and therapy. Created and documented by Michael White and David Epston more than 30 years ago, the Narrative practices and work were born out of a need to interact with therapy clients in a respectful and collaborative way. Most of these clients had been rendered voiceless, labelled with conditions that they were not asked to describe or name in their own words, even though they were living with these experiences every day.

Now the work engages in transformational ways with teams, organisations and communities, as a new generation of trained narrative practitioners brings these ideas into the mainstream.

The Narrative work begins with the idea that a word opens a world. We live in a world where how we speak, what we speak and the stories we tell define and become who we are. The work creates distance from these stories that we call **dominant problem-saturated narratives**. We give the problem narrative a name. We explore the history of the story as well as how we influence and are influenced by the narrative. We examine how the **taken-for-granted ideas and beliefs** in a particular society inform and sustain the problem narrative.[6] The work continually looks for moments and relationships in our history where that problem narrative was not true, was not the whole truth or was not present. Those different moments and relationships become the seeds for exploring the alternative narrative. We then give this alternative narrative a name. We further explore the ideas, beliefs, skills, gifts and community that can support this alternative narrative.

The Narrative approach seeks to address and confront us with our relationship to freedom and authorship, as it invites us to live a life where our participation in our stories and in the world really matters. As we re-write the narratives we once held to be the truth – and the only truth – about our lives, we shift the future of our own lives and the communities we form part of.

TALKING NARRATIVE

What's in a word? A world!

The Narrative approach not only talks about the power and influence of language, but takes it seriously and is attentive to every word spoken and written. If a word creates a world, it calls on our ethical responsibility to be both wary of our speaking and always aware of what our speaking and use of language are creating.

---

6   Chapter three gives an extensive exploration of the meaning and effects of taken-for-granted ideas and beliefs.

It also calls us to be intentional about the words we speak and the language that carries words, because our speech acts are not innocent acts. They create and produce the world we live in.

I have been intentional in my invitation and inclusion of as many readers as possible through the choice of particular words, phrases and sentences. Sometimes I used a string of synonyms or descriptions in a sentence that might look like an overload of words meaning the same thing. My intention in using these "strings of words or sentences" is to allow different entry points for different readers into the text. Because human beings make meaning of their lives through interpretation, a series of words or sentences can open up the margins to include and invite as many people as possible into the conversation – and, in this case, the book.

In a Narrative conversation the language of the **storyteller** is prominent and valued as worthy of not only being listened to, but the **listener** also weaves the language of the storyteller into the questions and reflections. The language used by the storyteller is never frowned upon, but is respected and unpacked, so that the meaning is never taken for granted.

In addition, narrative practitioners dance with the words of the storyteller as separate from the person, not trapped within the body and life of the storyteller, but something the storyteller is in relationship with.

Within this understanding of the power of language and the worlds we construct through language, the Narrative approach introduces words that are not always grammatically acceptable, such as the use of the word ***knowledges*** to make explicit that human beings have multiple forms of knowledge in the art and skill of living life on this planet.

For all these reasons, narrative practitioners end up sounding funny and weird and their questions might sound something like this: If *Silent Servant* (the name of a problem story) led your life, where would it have led your life to? At the end of the book I include a glossary to draw attention to some of the distinctive words and meanings you will encounter in Narrative practice.

The language of the Narrative work is a coded insider idiom that has at its heart to change and challenge the way we engage with our fellow human beings, communities and the world we live in. The artistry of this coded use of language invites and reveals the re-authoring of the world. The language we use in the Narrative work, and also in this book, speaks of the kind of relationship we prefer in our conversations with individuals, communities and organisations. It is a way of speaking that creates connectedness, invitation, inclusion and respect for the different worlds people inhabit and are trying to make sense of.

THE PROBLEM STORY

As a society we have become used to, and are sometimes enslaved and trapped by, stories that have limited hope and are **thin descriptions** or conclusions of who we are.[7] We call these **problem stories**, because they set limits on what is possible in and for our lives, our communities and our institutions.

These problem stories are powerful because we think and are often led to believe they are true and fixed, and may be the only truth about who we are and can become. This leads to an experience of being stuck, as we start to see and take our identity from these problem stories. Examples of problem-saturated stories with such **identity conclusions** could be the dysfunctional team, fragmented communities, the anorexic girl, the hyperactive child and the depressed man.

Problem stories get their power from and are informed by the assumptions and beliefs that we take for granted about the world around us. They dominate our lives and invite us to become mere docile bodies. Examples are the dominant beliefs in the scarcity of life – what we have is not enough and good things are scarce; leaders determine the culture of those they lead; the streets downtown are dangerous; foreigners will take advantage of us; salespeople are all about the money; the competitive nature of mankind; the inevitability of war; and the belief that only certain elites are authorised to "know" and declare what is true. These taken-for-granted ideas and beliefs are communicated, supported and validated by authority figures, professionals, experts and the media.

In addition, these taken-for-granted beliefs and ideas keep life predictable and do not produce anything new. They hide their history, influence and impact on our lives as we shrug our shoulders and tell our friends, "That's just the way it is." Their power as beliefs lies in the fact that we do not seek to challenge or confront them because we do not know how (or have had no invitations) to examine their history, influence or direct impact on our lives. This commitment to and our acceptance of the way things are, together with our ignorance of the powerful effects these ideas have on our own and others' life narratives and participation in this world, are part of what causes so much suffering and hopelessness.

Our fascination with problem stories and the accompanying abdication from participation have created a world that

- is not liveable for all[8]
- is in a relational crisis as we struggle to embrace the diversity of anyone who is different from us in any way
- has little understanding of and appreciation for the idea that we are one human race/kind and that collectively we are writing the story of our world
- tells single stories that are thin descriptions of who we are and what we can become

---

7   Geertz, C 1973. Thick Description: Toward an Interpretive Theory of Culture.

8   Walter Brueggemann interview with Krista Tippet: http://nearemmaus.com/2011/08/06/walter-brueggemann-interviewed-by-krista-tippett/

- values and validates the voices of experts and the media, which often discount the knowledges and wisdom that so-called ordinary human beings bring[9]
- has equated human beings to machines and producers of goods, product and profit
- has failed us and therefore we have to control this uncontrollable "machine" and "fix" what can be fixed while there still is time.

CHALLENGING OUR COMPLACENCIES

In my work I have seen a need for ways of being and living in this world that again access and promote the aliveness and possibility that would wake us up out of our sleep of complacency, blame and docility. Exploring how to live this life, how to make sense, how to participate, how to shift the narrative, how to hand in our abdication and resignation of this world from the so-called safety of our privatised individual worlds, is the intent and purpose of this book.

Narrative work, as I see it, challenges our complacency with the world we live in, our commitment to the way things are and our handing over of individual and communal narratives to people we authorise to speak and have a say in our lives and thinking. The Narrative approach aims to address all beliefs, ideas and practices that are abusive and confining, and mute human beings into docility and numbness. The approach exposes how the **tentacles of problem stories** have wrapped around our lives and brought the experience of futility to all our efforts.[10] The Narrative work invites **participants** in the process to take a position on, and differently position themselves toward, the problem stories that might have made sense to them and worked for them at some point, but now are mostly habits that have real effects in their lives.[11]

The work brings the gift of curiosity and questions to shine a light on the problem stories we hold about self, one another and the world. Often these questions enable us to realise how weary we have become of the problem stories that are not the preferred stories we have in mind for our own and our communal lives.

The Narrative approach provides transformative practices in being, listening and questioning that open up stories and understandings that we never imagined possible. This book provides ways to firstly become aware of the problem stories we participate in, and to help us see what our participation has cost us. It extracts

---

9 Whenever I refer to the multiplicity of knowledge in the skills and actions of living our lives, I refer to "knowledges" in the plural.

10 The term "tentacles of the problem story" explains the extent to which this story has affected or taken over various aspects of our lives, such as our relationships, our identities, and also work and the body.

11 Narrative practices work from the idea that we journey together and participate jointly in the conversation and re-writing of our stories. Therefore the word "participant" can refer to workshop participants, but mostly it describes the storytellers and listeners in the Narrative process.

us from the clutches and shackles of problem stories, changing our relationship with and to these stories. Problem stories inform our individual and communal identities, and when we are separated or distanced from them it creates a conversation where the alternative narrative is invited to be a rich part of our lives. Participants are then transported as they peek into a possible future they never thought likely.

THE POSSIBILITY OF THE NARRATIVE LENS

The Narrative approach creates a lens through which we might look at our stories with the knowledge that our world is created through language and in relationships.[12] It is an extraordinary kind of looking that opens up the possibility that the world is not as fixed as we have been taught. The **alternative story** is possible when a realisation is co-constructed that reality is fluid, that it can be challenged and changed, and transformed and lived into. The Narrative approach is an invitation to participate in this world, knowing that every word spoken, every act and every choice creates something.

Secondly, Narrative-informed conversations do not engage in the us/them divisive language so often used when we are looking for someone to blame. The Narrative work taps into the collective wisdom of groups, communities and nations, as collaboratively they challenge and stand against the problem stories they may have had a hand in creating and sustaining. This "standing together" taps into a communal transformative power, because it grows from rich histories, gifts and competencies that can create a new future.

THE ALTERNATIVE

Speaking about and participating in the problem stories of our own lives and those of the world we live in are easier to do, even though speaking and participating have huge implications for our lives. This book offers a means to shift and transform our relationship with our narratives, as participants discover that the problem story is not the whole truth about who they are. Narrative practices work from the idea that we journey together and participate jointly in the conversation and the re-writing of our stories.

Our lives are full of rich histories, skills, knowledges, relationships and alternative narratives that are waiting to be acknowledged and sometimes are already finding their way into a more prominent place in our lives. Who we are is constructed as we speak with and relate to others. Many people's lives go unsaid, unspoken, un-narrated. The Narrative work presents the gift of respect for the uniqueness of our diverse humanity. In addition, it opens the rich treasure chest of the multiplicity of stories and meanings that construct our identities. To a certain extent it allows and imagines what is possible not only for our own lives, but also for the relationships, communities and nations we are part of. The Narrative approach

---

12 The Narrative work is informed by the social constructionist ideas and approach, as promoted by the Taos Institute: http://www.taosinstitute.net/

engages the community in documenting, enriching and expanding an alternative vocabulary and an alternative world.

Re-Authoring Our World

The book is an invitation into the transformative Narrative process that opens the possibility of becoming agents and authors of our stories and our world. It gives an opening into an alternative future and narrative about God, the world, our work, community and neighbour, in addition to self. These alternative narratives are not prescribed or recommended by experts, but rather grow out of the rich histories, gifts and relationships of human beings, communities and organisations.

When we are confronted with the possibility of participating in our own stories, we are also confronted with our participation in this world. This invitation to participate then becomes a first step in re-authoring not only the web of collective stories we form part of, but also the possibility of re-authoring the world. The word 're-author' means that every individual, group, team, community and nation is a living author and participant in this world.

Sometimes we hand over the authorship or storytelling rights to our stories to those whom we have been taught to have respect for, sometimes at all cost, and we never question the effect of their ideas or practices. These taken-for-granted ideas and beliefs invite us into acceptance and voicelessness in a world that knows more about our lives and contexts than we can ever know.

Setting ourselves up as authors goes beyond merely thinking in a new way about our lives; it invites us to take up the pen or the brush and start writing or painting our lives and systems in new and preferred ways of being in this world. The Narrative approach invites us into the possibility of re-authoring our lives and producing communal and organisational stories in ways that speak to and of our reconstruction of what it means to be human during these times. The goal of this book is to provide the means for a conversation that invites human beings back into life and aliveness, as the re-authorising of lives and worlds opens up the possibility of imagining and creating a different world that has the common good of all our planet's inhabitants in mind.

The Narrative practices facilitate a way of being in this world where every conversation you enter into carries with it the possibility of transformation. These practices provide a way of seeing and being with other humans that, in itself, creates an alternative narrative that

- invites human beings into the abundance and multiplicity of stories, meanings, communities and possibilities
- creates a liveable world where every narrative shifting into life and breath is an exponential drop in the ocean of what we call planet Earth.

In creating a new future, those who participate in Narrative work have their eyes wide open for the multiplicity of alternative stories of abundance. Narrative work advocates breath and life in the sometimes unliveable world of anxiety and competition, because therein lies the art of living.

This book is an invitation to participate as prophets and poets who challenge the foundational language and assumptions that create wars, segregation and abdication, by awakening us into our transformative connectedness as human beings. This awakening re-authorises the individual narrative that spills over into re-authorising communal, national and international narratives, as we cannot but join hands in making this a liveable planet for us all.

There is a need in our world to open up ways of living where freedom and choice can lead to liberation. When we are provided with a transformative lens and practices, we are better able to see abundance and live from it. I believe an alternative narrative is already emerging and beckoning us to notice and thicken it.

PART I

NARRATIVE WORK AS A WAY OF BEING

*We cannot but see our worlds through the lens of the multiplicity
of our life and cultural stories. Within this understanding there are
no neutral, objective observers who are untouched by their life,
their world and the meaning that they have made of both. Being
aware, living, leading, consulting and coaching from your preferred
alternative life narrative re-authors the worlds that you enter.*

An important step in understanding Narrative work is to let it flow through your own life as you construct the story of your work and life. Within the Narrative approach we are aware that the multiplicity of our life stories serves as a lens that allows us to see and not see certain things. I see my work, life and clients through my eyes and through the stories of my own life, culture and context.

Knowing and naming the stories that inform my life help me to see when problem stories and alternative stories show up. As narrative practitioners we are always aware that as we dance between the multiplicities of our stories, we are in constant conversation with them. Our lives become a living text and a rich tapestry of and for the work when we name our stories, understand what kind of relationship we have with them, explore their history and influence, and are aware of the taken-for-granted beliefs and ideas that inform them. The thickening and enriching of the preferred alternative narratives of our lives propel us into a new future that is ideally supported and celebrated by a community of people (whether this be family members, friends and/or wider community networks and groups) who are seldom surprised about the choices we make and the life we pursue.

Apart from the lens of our own life stories, we are also gifted with the uniqueness, locality, contextuality and diversity of our culture and our nation's rich history, experiences, beliefs and values.

The Narrative approach is not something I do for companies or individuals; it is a way of being with them. This work and my stories are my companions in every conversation and community that I am invited to enter. As I am writing from this understanding of 'being with', I invite you into the stories, the communities and the contexts that inform my work and enable me to write what I am authoring and re-authoring at this specific time in my life.

CHAPTER ONE

THE NARRATIVES OF SELF

Within the multiplicity of stories that inform our lives and acts
of living, some narratives take over and start to dominate. This
dominant problem-saturated story then closes down the richness
of identity and living, resulting in thin conclusions about one's
identity. And yet, the alternative narrative is always present,
patiently waiting to be seen, to be invited back more fully into
the preferred way of living and being.

In reading the work of Michael White I was struck by the following question and answer: "What's in a word?[13] Answer – a world!" A couple of years ago I was overwhelmed by and trapped in a world for which I did not have the language. I did not even know that I could name this world. As an interpreting being I wove incidents together in a string of meaning, unaware that the knowledge and power of others – particularly that of my own culture and religious community – were informing and determining much of what I was able to see and name.

A friend introduced me to the Narrative work and I willingly and desperately offered my story so that I could understand this kind of therapy. A process began whereby I named the dominant problem story of my life, which had several other offerings before I felt that the *Silent Servant* was an appropriate name and description for this narrative.[14] This dominant problem narrative is one story that I have been in a relationship with for a long time.

A string of incidents that I interpreted, birthed and sustained the story of *Silent Servant* in my life. When I was about ten years old, my mom was working full-time and my dad took me aside and asked me to help out as the other woman in the house. On that day the story of the *Silent Servant* was born, and for most of the following 32 years I sustained this story, never thinking I could question or resist it. I thought it was the only way things are and could be, and tried my best to live up to the promises that I had made. I helped and supported my mother as promised, sometimes to the extent that I would not have enough time for my homework or did not sufficiently prepare for a test. School holidays were spent doing the laundry, ironing, cooking and cleaning, and on Saturdays I would help my mom clean the house.

---

13 White, M 1991. Deconstruction and Therapy.

14 In the Narrative work, when we have named a story, we capitalise the title in all forms of documentation. In this way we both honour the naming and distance the title from the person/ team or community. This shows that the person stands in a relationship to the story and its title.

THE WORLD OF *SILENT SERVANT*

The life and world of *Silent Servant* are supported by various taken-for-granted ideas and beliefs. My Afrikaner Christian culture validated *Silent Servant* as the way a girl-child should honour and respect her parents and show that a woman's work is to care for the men and children. Furthermore, a good woman is silent, she does not express her discontent about anything and she does not differ from a man – especially in public. These taken-for-granted beliefs and ideas that supported the life and the story of *Silent Servant* are based in the ideal of feminine goodness that believes in selfless care for others and does not include the nurturing of one's own life. Such ideas of feminine goodness can survive only in a culture of patriarchy, where the man is seen as the ruler of the household and the norm for how things should be done and thought of.

For a time, there were numerous benefits deriving from living into the story of *Silent Servant.* When I was a child, this story made me feel like a grown-up because I was affirmed as responsible, dependable and independent. Adults trusted me to look after smaller children and would reward me with gifts or take me out to dinner. This dependable good girl was also granted the privilege of sitting in the presence of adults when they had conversations while other children were told to go and play outside. Adults told me that all this serving was making me independent and teaching me valuable lessons. *Silent Servant* served me well.

As I grew older, *Silent Servant* was always on the lookout to serve and patiently waited for the recognition that came with it. The story of *Silent Servant* continued to play a role when I was studying at university, as I cooked and did the laundry for my male theology friends. In every act of service I was doing it for God, in a certain sense serving Him.

When I married, *Silent Servant* was very comfortable in her role as she knew exactly what she had to do and be. In my culture I received a lot of recognition for living into this narrative, and as the acknowledgement grew, the story spread its tentacles into most aspects of my life, my relationship with myself and my family. My religious community expected the *Silent Servant* and affirmed a wife who supported her husband, looked after our children and was part of his success story. In addition, I was often referred to as my husband's wife and not by my name. I became not only the *Silent Servant*, but sometimes the silent nameless servant. This is quite appropriate in the world of slavery, where the slave takes on the name of the slave master. *Silent Servant* invested her life in my husband's work, to the point that I had no sense of who I was and what was important to me.

My body started to rebel at the pace that this narrative was serving others – especially when I invited a family to come and live with us in our house. The lie that *Silent Servant* sold was that it was actually possible to serve and give your life away in this manner without any consequence to your identity, body and relationships. *Silent Servant* could go on and on serving in the name of God, but Chené was a human being who grew tired and eventually suffered from glandular fever, an underactive thyroid and high cholesterol. So, the foolishness that this narrative sold was that I could do it, I could be the *Silent Servant*, renounce any needs, be happy while doing it, fulfilled, a *skroplap* (Afrikaans word for dish rag) with joy.

THE FALL

Soon the fall was imminent. Gradually and continuously the life that *Silent Servant* had in mind for me no longer made sense, as I felt that I had ceased to exist. Incidents started to take place that made me feel I was not good enough and what I did was not good enough. *Silent Servant* would then convince me that I should not question anything or make a fuss, as it was my Christian and wifely duty to serve, and to do it joyfully and silently. A growing uneasiness with the way things were constructed gave rise to situations where I had to choose once again whether this was still the story I wanted to live into. It is like the tide going out and leaving you standing on dry ground, unsure of what to be or do – the tide of the problem story of the rule of *Silent Servant* was going out; it no longer made sense.

One day I did the inconceivable. I spoke up in a meeting and dared to challenge and question things. In a world that valued silence as goodness and dismissed speech as selfish, I had done the unthinkable. After I had spoken, I was told by the leader's wife that I was the axe against the tree of our religious community. When this comment was made, something came undone in my story and I found myself lying on my bed in a fetal position. It was the first time in my life that I had felt so hopeless. My husband was sent to fetch me and I had to return to the meeting, after which I was told to seek urgent psychological help. On that day the story of the *Silent Servant* was given a serious blow as I realised that in this story, Chené was not allowed to speak, to question or to challenge anything. She was only allowed to serve, and had to do it joyfully and silently. Up until that moment I had thought I was doing the right and good thing, giving my life away for my family, my religious community and my God.

On this day the tide of the dominant narrative went out from this once-familiar identity called the *Silent Servant*. I was tired of being misunderstood and measured by some invisible standard. I was tired of the loneliness. I was tired of the self-surveillance of my life as I tried to live up to some unspoken code of behaviour that I was measured by, subjugating myself to the image of the good woman, wife and mother. That day I made a sacred promise to myself that I would pursue a new life where Chené would be invited to live and speak, uninterrupted and unmuted.

Although this incident had a huge impact on my relationship with *Silent Servant,* I had not yet named the problem narrative. My life turned into a confusing journey in which I constantly saw myself as the problem, and was also told by powerful authority figures in my religious community that I was indeed the problem. For a few years I grew even more silent as I became weary of being judged when I did speak. The sacred promise that I had made to myself sometimes appeared as a faint whisper from another world.

And so it was time to position myself in terms of this dominant narrative and identity of which I was the author, although my narrative was largely authorised by others. I gave away the storytelling rights of my story to my religious community, my family and other women who seemed to know what a real, religious, Afrikaner woman should be doing and saying. I was isolated from the community, at odds with my own identity, and the trappedness left me hopeless. Chené could not remember what she liked anymore or why she was in this world apart from being in service to her husband, her children and her God. *Silent Servant* made me feel that this was all I was. This was it.

NAMING THE ALTERNATIVE NARRATIVE

The Narrative approach provided me with the means to name and make meaning of my world in a non-judgemental way. In the process of naming my narrative, *Silent Servant* was positioned in a space and place where I could look at her for the first time, as separate from myself. Initially I thought the distancing from the problem narrative was breaking some sacred code of a story that was supposed to be owned and lived forever, as my lot in life. That which had become my identity now became a thin description of what I showed up for in this world, an incomplete story. This impoverished narrative did not speak of the ravishing qualities of the gifts, visions, values, hopes and possibilities I wanted to live into. It had no intention of my showing up in the world as separate from this dominant identity known as *Silent Servant*.

Through a series of Narrative conversations with my friends and supervisors at the Institute for Therapeutic Development, and through the writing of my Master's and doctoral dissertations, I could gradually see myself as separate from this *Silent Servant* **constructed story** and identity. Powerful questions constantly interrogated this story's place in my life. One day my supervisor asked me, "What are you teaching *Silent Servant*?" Up until that point I had not thought that I could teach or was teaching *Silent Servant* anything. I thought I was *Silent Servant*; I had taken this identity into myself.

Questions like these became scaffolds that helped me enter the constellation of long-forgotten incidents and memories that told a different story. As I started to explore the exceptions, the times when *Silent Servant* was not all there was to my story, a wealth of incidents where I was leading and speaking in boldness, unafraid of being called 'the axe', came to the fore. Those exceptional stories were linked to a strong call I had felt as an agent and creator of transformation in this world while still in primary school. In addition, I could remember people who would talk about and testify to these moments of voice and transformation. I remembered how in my late high school years I arranged an ecumenical church service (something unheard of in my denomination at the time) between two religious denominations with differences in language and dogma that continue to this day. I fearlessly led prayer meetings and talks, and was acknowledged for the gifts I brought. I again began to access my dreams of being part of a world that could be transformed, and knew I had a role to play as *The Voice of Transformation in This World!*

This naming of the alternative narrative reconnected me with the call I felt in my participation in this world, as well as emphasising that it would no longer be through silent service, but through voice and transformation. Both my dissertations became documents that spoke of voice and transformation. As I entered the corporate world and started my own business, I discovered that just like at school, there was no place for the *Silent Servant.* When I named my business "Transformations", it formed part of this alternative narrative as I could celebrate it fully catching up with the alternative preferred story.

ENRICHING THE ALTERNATIVE NARRATIVE

The separation of my identity from the problem story and the movement into the alternative narrative has been a slow, sometimes painful, steady process. Three years ago I decided to board a plane to attend and present Narrative workshops in Canada and America. This was not an easy decision, but one my community – who had journeyed with me into the alternative narrative here in South Africa – urged and supported me to undertake. This choice accelerated the **counter-story** of *The Voice of Transformation in This World*, pushing it to another level.[15] I chose not to stay, nurture, serve and help, but instead chose to save the only life I could save – my own.

In the four weeks I spent in the Northern Hemisphere, I encountered communities that treated me differently than what I was accustomed to. During this journey abroad, the taken-for-granted beliefs and ideas of femininity and patriarchy were nowhere to be found in the conversations I entered. I felt I was being treated as a human being, not a woman, an object, a provider of services, but somebody with knowledges, skills and gifts who was participating in this world. I was asked to speak, and often I was asked to speak up. I felt like an equal, a beautiful woman with a brain and something to share with this world. The miracle of leaving my culture for four weeks and experiencing support and understanding for my alternative narrative, *The Voice of Transformation in This World*, has been pivotal in the re-writing and re-authoring of the counter-story of transformation that I am now living into.

Needless to say, it was chaos when I returned, for people in my family and culture were expecting *Silent Servant* to show up, and the Chené who returned from this trip was much too talkative. When you return to the familiar worlds after such a journey of transformation, you feel so lost. It is like going to a house where you are supposed to know where to find the milk and sugar, and you still do, but you don't know if you like milk and sugar anymore, or if you want to fetch them when somebody asks you. The re-writing and re-authoring of our stories indeed have real effects and serious consequences for every relationship and context we stand in.

---

15 "Counter-story" is a term Hilde Lindemann Nelson uses in her book *Damaged Identities, Narrative Repair*. She describes counter-stories as "tools designed to repair the damage inflicted on our identities by abusive power systems" (2001:xiii). I use "counter-stories", "counter-narratives" and "counter-files" interchangeably when referring to stories and files that are counter to the cultural or problem-saturated stories spoken and told by the dominant taken-for-granted ideas and beliefs in our society, through its advocates.

SAYING GOODBYE

The freedom that I subsequently chose to live into meant I no longer showed up as *Silent Servant*, doing for my family what they could do for themselves. Maybe I was just no longer so arrogant as to think I was capable of such serving acts anymore. This newfound freedom came to unsettle everything I had taken for granted in my world. The gift of seeing my identity and my life through a new set of eyes was scary for everyone.

And so the time came for me to let the story of *Silent Servant* go. I was not sure what kind of ritual would be appropriate to complete this narrative, as one cannot drop the story in an instant: to do so would be an act of violence to the people who knew the story in a particular way. How could I honour this narrative which, towards the end, was entrenched in so much grief? In a conversation with Angeles Arrien we decided that *Silent Servant* did not need a funeral, but rather an acknowledgment of her hard work.[16] We also decided that *Silent Servant* was really tired and needed to be sent on a nice boat cruise for at least a year; she would appreciate the rest and the treat.

On 21 December 2010, I held a small ceremony with a few friends in San Francisco Bay to thank and honour *Silent Servant* for her role in my life story. I said good-bye on a very special winter solstice night, with a total eclipse of the moon participating in this important ritual. I acknowledged *Silent Servant* and her contribution to the preceding 32 years of my life:

- She taught me how to work hard and relentlessly, sometimes without pause or rest
- She always kept her word and would hurt herself in keeping her promises
- She entered into and opened up relationships in service of others
- She took away the fear of adults
- She laid the foundation for my character
- She taught me to pay attention to other people's needs
- She taught me how to really listen.

On this night an Amaretto was an appropriate drink to toast *Silent Servant*, as it represented the bittersweet flavour constructed in this narrative. The ritual brought both sadness and relief all at once. I was left with a sense of freedom, a readiness and eagerness to take up the pen and start writing in a newly enthused way.

16 Angeles Arrien is a cultural anthropologist, award-winning author, educator and consultant to many organisations and businesses. She lectures and conducts workshops worldwide, bridging cultural anthropology, psychology and comparative religions. Her work is currently used in medical, academic and corporate environments. She is President of the Foundation for Cross-Cultural Education and Research. Her books have been translated into 13 languages and she has received three honorary doctorate degrees in recognition of her work. http://www.angelesarrien.com/

In my culture and family the call and longing for *Silent Servant* to return will always be there. Although I have officially let her go, she still comes to visit. When I give a talk, I sometimes say I am sorry as I apologise for speaking or saying too much. I still struggle to fully embrace the needs and longings I have as legitimate and important. Life in service of and to others is so much easier to see as legitimate and important.

The moment I named the alternative narrative, a new world was invited in. As I whispered the birth of the naming of an alternative story, an alternative world and life opened up. *The Voice of Transformation in This World* became more richly described as a diverse group of people formed a **community of concern** around the alternative narrative. A beautiful community of black brothers and sisters, who facilitated with me in the Personal Change programme at AngloAmerican Platinum, joined in this story by taking my hand and teaching me how not to be a *skroplap*, but to live into the strong, resonant voice of the alternative narrative.[17] A loving gay community of friends helped me to dress beautifully, eat well and celebrate every milestone with rituals they took part in. In North America, various individuals and groups like A Small Group in Cincinnati were available to help me see and continuously challenge all the taken-for-granted ideas that *Silent Servant* advocated and validated. As a result, the alternative narrative, in all its bareness and fragility, has been patiently held, nurtured and enriched by a community of concern – a group of people who are not surprised that *The Voice of Transformation in This World* is the alternative narrative into which I am now living and writing, especially as I wrote this book.

What sustains me in living the alternative narrative are the continuous reminders from this wonderful community of concern regarding the gifts, commitments, values and possibilities that I bring to this world. This community has become my village, cheering me on as I still wander at times in the wilderness, overwhelmed by the voices of my culture and others that I have authorised to speak over so many years. I am continuously provided with the space where *The Voice of Transformation in This World* can live into and be heard as the narrative is more "richly and thickly described."[18] What a breath-taking journey of preferred ways of becoming not the self-made woman, but a woman held by the **rich descriptions** and tender loving care of a community which continuously and relentlessly supports the counter-story and questions the thin conclusions that the dominant problem story brought.

17 For background on the Personal Change programme at AngloAmerican Platinum, see http://www.angloplatinum.com/sus/eco/people_development.asp

18 White, M & Epston, D 1990. *Narrative Means to Therapeutic Ends*, p. 13.

PART II

INVITATIONS TO RE-HUMANISE

Narrative practices grow from the ground of seeing and understanding the world in a way that acknowledges a rich multiplicity of stories of humanity, identity and community.

In the movie *Patch Adams* a medical professor says to his first-year class: "We are here to train your humanity out of you and turn you into something better; we are going to make doctors out of you!" This explanation of the human quest and view of the modern age articulates the de-humanising project of our Western world.[19] It explains a knowing and judgement about human beings and human nature, focused on their fragility, fallibility, weaknesses, deficiencies, unpredictability and unreliability.[20] All of these qualities are somehow trapped in our bodies and need to be trained out of us by medical professors, teachers, parents, pastors, therapists and leaders.

In our quest to rise above our own untrustworthy humanity, the only hope given to us is from examples of messiah-type figures such as Mother Teresa, Gandhi, Nelson Mandela and Martin Luther King. It appears that they could somehow 'beat' their own humanity and all its tendencies, although we also get the "behind-

---

19 "Western culture", which is sometimes equated with Western civilisation or European civilisation, is used very broadly to refer to a heritage of social norms, ethical values, traditional customs, religious beliefs, political systems, and specific artefacts and technologies. The term has come to apply to countries whose history is strongly marked by European immigration or settlement, such as the Americas and Australasia, and is not restricted to Western Europe: http://en.wikipedia.org/wiki/Western_culture

I intentionally chose to cite Wikipedia for some of the descriptions of terms discussed here. In doing so, I take a stand on crowd-sourced language, meaning and knowledges as having an equal voice in describing the world we live in. In addition, I found these so-called un-authoritative sources richly languaging what I wanted to say.

20 These reflections were inspired by an article by Michael White on the limitations of seeing certain qualities as properties of human nature that lead to expressions of wonder, yet end up being thin descriptions of the lives we live: http://www.psybc.com/pdfs/library/WHITE.pdf

the-scenes real life story" to comfort us. Even these people were human, after all. Whenever human beings get it right, they have strengths, resources, inner drive, ambition, authenticity and competencies and have done enough "work" to now live from these qualities that they equally own.

The effect of these ideas is that they set us up against one another. We do not seem to be equally endowed with strengths and resources. We are isolated from one another, as the success of my strengths and resources will get me the job I want and I have to make sure that the employer sees that I am the ideal candidate for the job. It renders invisible the context, effect of power and the uniqueness and multiplicity of our lives and knowledges of living. This way of thinking fosters competition and judgement, and measures success by the amount of visible strengths and resources and by how obviously we overcome the dark side of our humanity to achieve results that matter in this world.

In addition, we have come to believe that if we distance ourselves from our own and others' humanity, we will be better able to help others. We have therefore acquired ways of speaking about others with labels, so that we are left feeling no connection to them as human beings. Speaking about people by using labels turns human beings into objects that can be analysed, judged and scrutinised. Examples of such labels are 'feminist', 'rebellious teenager', 'gay nurse', 'homeless man', 'negative team', 'unethical organisation', 'poor community' and 'violent nation'.

The Narrative work acknowledges that through the ages human nature has been defined in various ways, and may constantly be redefined. In our lifetime, I believe that the Narrative practices are relevant as they take us out of the stuck debate and story about human nature, and offer us a way of seeing our humanity that opens up new possibilities of re-authoring and re-writing what this means.

In South Africa, Zulu people greet one another with "Sawubona", which means, "I see you" or "Sanibonani" which means "We are seeing you". It is a greeting that acknowledges the other person as a human being to be seen and valued. This greeting also acknowledges that when I greet you, I greet you with the rich history, community and legacy that have shaped and informed me. When we use this greeting we answer with the words "Yebo, sawubona", which means "Yes, I see you". The Narrative work grows from an understanding that when we are seen in our humanity we challenge the beliefs and ideas that de-humanise and objectify us as human beings.

Narrative work proposes a different way of participating with and seeing that speaks of

* human beings as storying beings
* human beings as interpreting beings
* human beings as knowledgeable beings
* human beings as languaging beings
* human beings as re-authoring beings

- human beings as human becomings
- human beings as communing beings
- human beings as gifted beings
- human beings as transformational beings[21]
- re-humanising the world through the telling, re-telling and witnessing of the multiple stories of our lived experiences – stories that we have interpreted and stories that we are knowledgeable about
- re-naming our world by using our own language in the titles of our narratives
- re-authorising our world and lives by being aware of challenging and resisting the taken-for-granted beliefs and ideas of people we authorise and hand the pen over to in the writing of our lives
- re-dreaming a life, world and future through alternative narratives as we live into a different direction beyond what we have taken for granted
- re-communalising a world that is trapped in individualism and isolation by allowing a community of co-journeyers to walk alongside us
- re-gifting our world by receiving and giving **gifts** abundantly, as we allow a community of co-journeyers to see and name what we are not always able to.

The philosophical approach and values of the Narrative work grow out of a groan or cry for respectful ways of being with our fellow human beings, where collectively we can make this a liveable world for all.

The chapters in part two explain the "why" of the work, so that when we come to part three, you will understand the beautiful flowers that emerge from this fruitful soil. This section will explore the roots and ground from which the Narrative approach grows, to explain why we use these practices and what it means when we name the practices in a particular way.

The Narrative work gives you a lens to see

- human beings
- the multiplicity of stories of societies
- the possibility of an alternative future.

Distinctions will also be provided to help you navigate through the inherent meanings found in the Narrative ideas and practices, in instances where meanings and phrases sound the same.

---

21 Thank you to Fungiwe Dlakavu for drawing my attention to human beings as transformational beings.

CHAPTER TWO

SANIBONANI TO HUMAN BEINGS

Narrative practices seek to re-humanise the world through the telling, re-telling and witnessing of the multiple stories of our lived experience – stories that we have interpreted and stories that we are knowledgeable about. The work also re-names our world by using our own language in the titles of our narratives.

We live in a Western world that often sees stories as the domain of children, part of the jokes we tell around the kitchen table and the practices of indigenous cultures. Storytelling is not something serious human beings do in the real world. In the quest to colonise and develop this world, we have lost track of the way we make sense and meaning of our world through stories. We have languaged our world in facts, memorandums and policies that would make our lives certain and predictable.

This chapter is an invitation to re-write and re-author our relationship to the multiplicity of stories we live by every day. It is an invitation to draw life and aliveness out of the procession of the living dead. It is an invitation to reconnect to our humanity, where faith and mystery reappear in the resurrection of the multiplicity of stories.

HUMAN BEINGS AS STORYING BEINGS

The Narrative approach believes that human beings make meaning of their lives through the stories they tell. We live within the multiplicity of stories that are co-constructed with other human beings, and our ancestors and the histories they have handed us. When we see human beings as storying beings, we know that everything that happens has the potential to be interpreted, storied and told.

In this work, a narrative is seen as the end result of a meaning-making process where certain incidents are woven together in a story. There is a multiplicity of stories and meanings, all running concurrently, about who we are and what we can become that informs our identity and actions as human beings. In my case, along with the stories of *Silent Servant* and the *Voice of Transformation*, there are also the narratives of the Music Teacher, the Olympic Athlete, the Cool Mother, the Seeker of Spirituality, and more. These narratives are all informed by my **meaning making** of various events and incidents, the taken-for-granted beliefs and ideas of my culture and society that have influenced the conclusions I have drawn about my identity and what actions are therefore possible in my life.

In the Narrative approach the narratives told by human beings are seen and valued for their uniqueness within their particular context and culture. We believe narratives speak of our individual and communal identity which is co-created in our relationships with other people, our history and our culture. We are always mindful that a whole constellation of narratives plays out at the same time, and the understanding of identity is cast in the narrative structure of life and communal stories.

This work starts from the insight that the narrative is something we have constructed. What people think is "true" and "their reality" we call a **constructed narrative**. A constructed narrative consists of a series of incidents which we have interpreted to say: "This is my story!" It seems true to the person who often refers to their story as "this is the way it is". In this understanding of the way things are, it is inevitable that as we live our narratives, our narratives become our way of living.

The Narrative work sees the narrative as the basic unit of experience and focuses on how and when these narratives are formed, how they influence human beings, how they are shaped by taken-for-granted ideas and beliefs, and how people and institutions authorise certain preferred stories and identities. The work also invites the possibility of alternative narratives into human beings' choice by exploring the gifts, hopes, values, dreams, beliefs, evidence and support of this narrative. It therefore opens up the possibility for human beings to choose again which of these narratives they prefer to live into, how they want to stand in relationship to the narrative, and which narratives they prefer to be re-written, more richly described and transformed.

The intention of Narrative practices is to invite human beings to become agents and authors who are able and gifted to paint or write a new preferred narrative, or live into a story that has already started but is merely hidden, thinly described or incomplete. In addition, the Narrative approach is a way of being that lives into our human becoming and appreciation thereof. The hope of this work lies in the possibility that if the narratives we live are constructed anyway, why not live into a narrative that is chosen and alive with possibility?

STORYTELLING AND NARRATIVE WORK

I have been in countless conversations over the years where the mention of the word "narrative" (as in Narrative approach), guides the conversation to the practice of storytelling. This section is an attempt at clarifying the difference between storytelling and Narrative work.

In most cultures, storytelling is an old practice whereby tales are told about a people's history, why things are the way they are, and why certain things are valued and affirmed. The act of storytelling in this context is used to teach and convey the facts, values and history, as perceived through the lens of that particular culture.

There is also a movement across the world to return to the ancient tradition of storytelling as a way to connect as human beings. These movements organise storytelling events during which the storytelling capacity of human beings is celebrated.

In addition, there are training workshops that teach people to construct their own life stories and to tell them as a way to raise funds, market new endeavours or promulgate new leadership initiatives. The aim is to tell good, compelling stories that "sell" a vision, strategy, business venture or product to employees or customers.

In these different understandings of the idea of storytelling, there is no movement in the storytelling itself. The stories are fixed and not open to be challenged, re-told or re-storied. These stories might even be seen as a fact, true and/or the way things are. Maybe this telling or the fixedness thereof can even be seen as an escape from the movement that is possible in the story.

Narrative work does not help people tell a compelling story or engage in storytelling for the sake of telling a story. The telling of the story in Narrative work serves as a springboard for the exploration of the multiplicity of stories, the multiplicity of meanings, ideas and relationships that inform the identity conclusions human beings have drawn from these stories. Because of human beings' interpreting ability, stories are seen as expressions of meaning making in language. In the Narrative work, stories are always unpacked, thickened, challenged, explored through questions and therefore always on the way towards making meaning and sense. These practices create the conversation from which invitations to thicken, re-author, re-write and transform the story are explored. In the exploration of people's stories, the Narrative work remains respectful of the cultural and communal stories (also called taken-for-granted beliefs and ideas) that inform people's lives and provide ways in which participants are able to look at the influence and history of these stories.

Human Beings as Naming Beings

As human beings we name our worlds from the age that we start to talk. As we name things at this young age, we usually make up words as we make sense of the world. Soon, adults, teachers, our friends and family members correct us by teaching us the "right" word or term for things. At some point we stop naming things in our own **experience-near**[22] language or **unlisted language**[23] and listen carefully to the right and approved language and way of speaking. This results in human beings avoiding having to name things differently, as they know they will be corrected, advised and sometimes even ridiculed, although some might call us poets or artists when we name things in the wonder with which we see them.

---

22 Experience-near language talks about expressions and experiences in our own words and in meaning making that is familiar to us. This is a term Stephen Madigan uses in the following article: http://therapeuticconversations.com/wp-content/uploads/2010/01/Handout_Madigan_Reauthoring_TC9-1.pdf

23 In an interview with Lynn Hoffman, "Aliveness and the Timeless Way of Helping", she introduces the idea of unlisted or hidden language that exists, but has not been qualified as a proper subject deserving of description. In the same way, people make meaning of their lives and name the stories they live by in language that might not be acknowledged or qualified as "proper". Unlisted language therefore opens up the possibility for the world to be named in a new way. See: http://www.youtube.com/watch?v=HUoZuEnoEkk&feature=youtu.be

The surveillance of our speaking and naming has a place in making us coherent in our daily conversations with one another, but this push to name experience with a template standardised by society can become the portal into accepting the **given world** and life as is.

The Narrative work provides an invitation to reclaim the naming quality of our humanity. As we name our worlds and stories, we are able to distance ourselves from them and the opportunity opens up for us to choose again whether or not this is the story we want to live into. In this regard the philosopher Ludwig Wittgenstein said: 'The limits of my language mean the limits of my world."[24] When we invite human beings to name their worlds and stories in their own language and understanding, they can open the limits and constraints of their worlds and decide again about the kind of relationship they want to have with these worlds and the stories that they have named. This naming quality helps human beings enter a world for which they have now created a language. I believe, like Wittgenstein, that "uttering a word [or a name that is owned] is like striking a note on the keyboard of the imagination".[25] Sometimes people find the first uttering of the name of their story extremely difficult, as the voice of society tends to push them to use the "right" word. When they find a name and title for their story that comes from their rich meaning making, it indeed strikes up the imagination of a whole symphony of notes, as the first note invites other stories to sing along.

HUMAN BEINGS AS INTERPRETING BEINGS

The words human beings use to describe their experience have been handed to them by what is socially or culturally acceptable, but when it comes to making meaning of experience, the multiplicity of meanings opens a whole other world. When narrative practitioners journey with participants, we always confirm what a word, however familiar, means for the storyteller.[26] In the Narrative work we do not believe in a one-size-fits-all approach which implies that when a person uses a word such as "anger", it means the same thing for all people, in every culture and generation, across all time. Again, we always clarify with questions: How do you understand this word? What does this mean for you? We never assume that we know what is meant, as in the telling and re-telling of a story a word can be showered with new meaning that is not yet told or expressed.

In addition to confirming the meaning of specific words, we also interpret actions and events. If we ask a group of people to tell the story of a video clip of events and incidents that has no text, we will most probably have as many interpretations as we have people telling the story of what really happened. Our multiplicity of arguments and diverse expressions in the stories we tell can only begin to help us understand the multiple ways the same video clip is interpreted.

---

24 Wittgenstein, L 1922. *Tractatus, Logico-Philosophicus*.

25 Wittgenstein, L 1953/2001. *Philosophical Investigations*.

26 When the word "storyteller" is used here, it refers to the individual, community or organisation that invites narrative practitioners on a co-journey. It does not refer to the quality of the story or the art of telling a story.

As human beings we cannot but interpret whatever happens to us or what happens in the world. There are multiple interpretations and understandings of what happens in individual and communal lives, and therefore the narrative is not fixed but always fluid, on the way of making sense and understanding. Narratives are constructed in language and are fictional in the sense that they are created through our interpretation and meaning making.

These multiple recollections of the past and present are indeed powerful because they shape people's experiences of their lives, identities, histories and futures. We construct our identities and our actions through the meaning we make of the narratives we tell about our lives, our work, our relationships, our organisations, our God(s) and our communities. We do not simply recount our stories, but we tell what happened from our understanding and the meaning we have created.

This meaning-making process is constructed in language and relationships and informed by taken-for-granted ideas and beliefs as well as cultural stories. These ideas and beliefs form another layer of meaning that enables us to say about our story, "This is just the way it is" and they can become limiting when we see them as based on so-called fixed realities.

We have no control over the interpretations and meaning human beings make about one another and the world we live in. We can, however, question the lenses and interpretations through which we see the world, and ask questions about them. This process might be scary as people discover how their once-familiar and certain worlds crumble under questioning. On the other hand, the experience of questioning our meaning making might also be liberating when people realise that the meaning they made was informed by powerful ideas and beliefs that are not cast in stone.

People's narratives are therefore always in motion and can change the moment new meaning is made and lived into.

THIN AND RICH DESCRIPTIONS

Certain stories, ideas and beliefs that are handed down to us through our cultures and societies can be either richly or thinly described. Thin descriptions of our conventional stories are very powerful, because they lure us into believing that they are the truth and that their roots or their influence on us are not up for questioning. Thin descriptions throw us into a simplistic right–left and a conservative–liberal way of speaking that creates an us-and-them and winner-and-loser conversation. Thin descriptions drive us apart as people, and leave no room for **the other**.[27]

By contrast, rich descriptions of stories, ideas and beliefs include their history, influence and power, and open up possibilities of being questioned, which again

---

27 When I use the term "other", it means any person who is different from me in any way with regard to race, gender, educational level, age, culture, economic status, etc. I sometimes use the word "stranger" as an alternative to "other".

opens up the possibility of choice. This is one of the gifts of the Narrative work: it engages us in thickening and enriching our language, in naming and meaning making. Rich descriptions open up the conversation to the uniqueness and extraordinary lives and actions of human beings that include the other.

Every conversation in the Narrative work is the text we work with. We richly describe that text through the kinds of questions we ask. The Narrative work opens a way for people, teams, organisations, communities and nations to think anew about what they are creating in the naming, telling and retelling of the stories they are wedded to, by asking questions that shift the conversation for us all.

HUMAN BEINGS AS KNOWLEDGEABLE BEINGS

In the Narrative work, practitioners are always aware that power relations exist and we cannot escape from them. These power relations are neither good nor bad, but have real effects on human beings and their interactions. Institutions, communities or individuals that are considered to have power and knowledge in a particular society often decide what real knowledge is, who can speak, who is worth listening to, what would be helpful to others, who is important, and where and how to spend resources.

These power relations benefit from our dependence on experts, leaders, teachers, professionals and government to think for us, decide for us, speak for us and, most important of all, label us.

In the world we live in, we have constructed strong divisions to categorise some human beings as knowledgeable, and others as objects and mere recipients of those who "really know". When we divide human beings into those who know and those who do not, we decide who can speak and who must remain silent. A language of labels has been created to keep the world aware of who knows and who does not and, as a result, who can speak and who should listen: teacher/ student; doctor/patient; leader/follower; educated/uneducated, etc. Even if we do acknowledge that those human beings who are mere recipients of some expert's knowledge (like students) might know something, we still decide whether their knowledge is legitimate and worth giving attention to.

Within the Narrative approach we see human beings as knowledgeable and as the **experts** in the life and communal stories they tell. The work of the narrative practitioner is to create the space and issue an invitation for participants to bring their knowledges, to value their knowledges and to legitimise those knowledges. This space is created through the way of being with storytellers, through the kinds of questions being asked, as well as the way in which knowledge is constructed together with the storyteller.

David Epston refers to these knowledges as **insider knowledges** that have the following qualities:

Insider knowledges are local, particular and at times unique as they often arise from imagination and inspiration, not the usual technologies of scientific knowledge-making. ... Because they are, in the first instance, the intellectual property or otherwise of the person(s) concerned, outsiders cannot rightly claim either invention or ownership of such knowledges. "Insider knowledges" are modest and make no claims beyond the person(s) concerned. They do not seek any monopolies of "knowing" but sponsor many kinds and ways of knowing. "Insider knowledges" do not provide grand schemes as they are far too humble for that ... and are carried best by and through stories. [28]

EXPERTS AND CO-JOURNEYERS

The way we see human beings determines what we expect from them and how we define our role as the ones who are listening. This relationship carries with it tremendous responsibility and power, because the one who knows and who is allowed to speak can open and close opportunities for participation in the relationship, as well as the possibilities that can flow from it.

Experts

In our Western society, we have constructed the idea of experts to mean that a person is a specialist in a certain area of knowledge, is acknowledged as an authority in that area, and can now charge professional fees for the expertise s/he provides. Experts within the area of the humanities, for example, are expected to show up in the world with knowledge and **truth claims** about other human beings and human nature (the client, individual, patient, company, organisation, community, nation, etc.), as well as knowing about the other and seeing the other as an object to guide, fix, correct and help. Within this understanding of expertise, the object of help and rescue does not know and does not have the resources to know. Even if human beings are seen as knowing something, their knowledges have to be weighed, legitimised, qualified, examined and then validated by these experts before they might be of any use.

Co-journeyers

The Narrative approach is always aware of power relations, and intentionally challenges them by taking the ostensibly ignorant wisdom and knowledges of storytellers as jewels, as moments at which to pause, to be recognised and asked about, never frowned upon or judged. The intention of Narrative practices is to firstly view the storyteller/community as a person/group with endless wisdom, knowledges and gifts in the art of living. Narrative practitioners position the storyteller or community as the expert in the telling. This positioning comes with a careful curiosity about the life, history and gifts that each storyteller brings to the conversation.

---

28   Hancock, F & Epston, D 2008. The Craft and Art of Narrative Inquiry in Organisations, pp. 485–486.

The task of the listener is to treat these insider knowledges as something worth giving attention to, asking about and listening to. As a result it challenges the idea that only certain people know, can talk and therefore have power in the speaking. Those who do not have a voice, because they do not know and are not allowed to speak, are given a voice as experts in this conversational space. These challenging questions and ways of being create a space where the storyteller can show up as the expert of their narrative and life. In the Narrative work, "the client is the expert"[29] means that the intention of the listeners is to ask questions of the storyteller-as-the-expert, always seeing that individual as the one who knows most about their own life.

Narrative practitioners see human beings as standing in relationship with a multiplicity of skills, gifts, commitments, values, hopes and dreams. We come alongside people with curiosity, respect and transformational questions that open up the possibilities of the not-yet-said and named alternative narrative that we assume is already present. As co-journeyers with people and communities, narrative practitioners, bring the art, of questioning and respect for the humanity of others who are seen and treated as knowledgeable experts. In this different way of being with one another we become one another's teachers in the journey of exploring and celebrating our own humanity.

HELPING AND JOINING

In the Western world people tend to call on experts whom they expect to fix whatever is broken, in exchange for money. The higher the price, the bigger the expectation regarding the kind of help and expertise that can be offered. A higher price might also include the expectation of a speedy delivery as well as a high expectation of the extent to which things that are broken can be mended and fixed.

Helping

Narrative practitioners believe that the idea of an expert "helping" human beings comes from an understanding of the person/community being helped due to limitations in their knowledge and resources. Within this understanding human beings need to be corrected and helped by those who know and have the resources: the experts. In this helping exchange, the person/community who is offered help is not expected to have a voice, to contribute or to have gifts and knowledges to bring to the table. Experts who offer help assume that the help they offer will be helpful because it comes from an understanding that what was good for them, or for somebody else, will also be good for the person/community being helped.

Joining

In the Narrative work we come alongside fellow human beings with the belief that they are the experts of their own lives and we, as listeners, are therefore open to be touched and taught by the storyteller. As joint partners the storyteller

---

29 Anderson, H & Goolishian, H 1992. The Client is the Expert...

and listener each brings richness to the conversation that transports both to a different place and space from when they entered the conversation.

Legitimising the knowledges that participants bring to the conversation, and mining them through the questions we ask, is very important in the Narrative process. Both the listener and the storyteller work together in the conversation, with one offering the expertise of questions and respectful being, and the other offering the expertise of a rich description of a life story that has been supported by numerous gifts, skills, commitments and a full history. In this understanding, knowledge is seen as something that the listener and the storyteller are constructing together.

The helping that occurs in this work is only considered "help" when the storyteller-as-the-expert qualifies that the conversation was indeed helpful.

NOT-KNOWING APPROACH

As Narrative practitioners we are conscious of where knowledge resides in a conversation. When people consult us, there is an expectation of the power of our expertise as narrative practitioners and the storytellers as people who should be listening, people who are not-knowing. When we use the Narrative approach, the knowledge and expertise we bring lie in using the text of the story and the language of the storyteller to ask questions about the meaning of words and ideas, even if they sound familiar and we think we know what they mean. We consult the storyteller-as-the-expert by adopting a not-knowing approach born out of curiosity.[30] In this way we decentre the power that is constructed within this context.

We work from a stance that at no time do we assume that we know what the person, community or organisation is talking about or trying to say. We always ask questions to which we do not know the answers and consult the storyteller- or community-as-the-expert with questions such as: What does it mean when you say that you want to live into a Festival story as a community?

HUMAN BEINGS AS AGENTS AND AUTHORS

Within the Narrative approach we do not see the person or community as the problem but understand that people stand distinct from and in relationship with the problems they face. Narrative practitioners believe that society focuses on the internalisation of problems (taking the problem inward or inside so that people/communities see themselves as the problem) to such a degree that the person becomes the problem.

The Narrative work does not locate problems within people or **totalise** people with labels related to their problems. Narrative practitioners do not talk in totalising or labelling language such as the "poor community", "fearful child", "over-protective

---

30 Anderson, H & Goolishian, H 1992. The Client is the Expert...

mother", and the like. We understand that there are problems, but we always look at the surrounding context and ask how it is that the person, team or community is taken over by the problem. The relationship people have with the problem is seen as the problem.

In addition we explore how the person, team and community are challenging, overcoming or resisting the problem. The problem therefore has an influence on people's lives, and the person or community influences the life of the problem.

So often the Narrative work is criticised when people hear that the approach does not see the person/team/community as the problem, but views the problem itself as a problem. Some feel that if you distance yourself from a problem, you may abdicate your involvement and participation in the problem story. Quite the opposite happens: when participants distance themselves from the problem narrative, they can see how the narrative has influenced their lives and how they have influenced the problem narrative. Seeing how the tentacles of the problem narrative have reached into certain areas of their lives, and not into other areas, opens up the possibilities for a problem narrative to not be all there is to life, to not be a single story of who we are. Choice and possibility open up.

The Narrative approach asks questions that invite storytellers to experience themselves as agents in this world. Once storytellers realise how their narratives are constructed, how they influence their lives and how they are informed by taken-for-granted ideas and beliefs, the question becomes whom they have authorised to speak in a powerful way about their narrative and identity. When these stories are richly described, storytellers are invited to choose what kind of relationship they want to have with the story, and are thus invited into accountability and responsibility. These invitations challenge the relationship storytellers have with the entrenched ideas and wishes of others that result in their being mere onlookers to the drama of their lives. Inviting people to re-tell these stories in a particular way is an invitation to authorship, to taking back the rights to the telling and writing of their stories. We say they are re-authoring their lives.

When we say "Sanibonani" we see and invite the richness of human beings as storying, interpreting, naming and knowledgeable beings to be seen in a different way in this world. This quality of seeing unlocks new worlds of being with one another that invite transformation for individuals and communities.

CHAPTER THREE

RE-AUTHORISE OUR WORLD

*Through Narrative practices we re-authorise our world and
lives by being aware of and challenging taken-for-granted
beliefs in our life and communal stories. We resist the harmful
ideas of people we authorise to write the narrative of our lives.
We take back the pen to re-authorise and re-author our world.*

TAKEN-FOR-GRANTED-BELIEFS AND IDEAS

Taken-for-granted beliefs are ideas in society and in our cultures that we grow up with and that strategic people in positions of authority tell us are the given world, the way things are, the fixed reality. "The way things are" describes a society or culture's construction of its perceived worldview, reality, values and way of life. It conveys messages of what is good and worthwhile and therefore constrains the possibility of choices. There is no opening for movement within these ideas and beliefs, nor is there any opportunity for an experience to move you, as taken-for-granted ideas and beliefs describe the experience only as a fact, a given.

Initially taken-for-granted ideas and beliefs might look strange and foreign to us, but they do not remain in the category of what "they say" for too long. If we hear these ideas and beliefs often enough, especially from people in society whose voices are valued as having authority, they are taken into our lives as we interpret and make meaning of what is given. We then internalise these ideas and they become part of our way of life and thinking, like a lens through which we see life and our own identities. This lens gives us limited vision, allowing us to see and not see certain things and to pay attention to what is worth paying attention to, as defined in this social and cultural construction.

These beliefs and ideas become so familiar and integrated into our lives that we no longer see them as foreign to the constellation of our stories. As they disguise their true nature, taken-for-granted ideas and beliefs inform and shape our stories, our identity conclusions, relationships and eventually also what is possible for our lives. They become an intrinsic part of life, the way things are.

These taken-for-granted ideas and beliefs are very powerful as they create a way for societies to judge whether human beings can be rewarded or should be condemned for following or resisting them. They also create a hierarchy in which some people are judged to be performing better within the construct of these ideas and beliefs than others. For example, there is a belief that if you work hard, you will succeed in life. Success would then equate to earning a decent salary that enables you to provide food for your family, a place to live, enough money to be able to travel and dress in a respectable manner. But when you are working hard (meeting the requirement of society) yet are not able to support a family within what society measures as success, the judgement starts: you are condemned for not having enough ambition to get a better job that might earn you more money or for not working hard in school so that you can go to university and earn a degree, for being a bad mother/father who cannot provide for the family, or for being poor and having the mindset of a poor person who always wants to be cared for by others, and so on. This example shows how these ideas and beliefs locate the problem within people and label them from this knowing about them; in the same breath it renders blind the economic and class systems that create the conditions that sometimes make it impossible for people to move beyond.

Further examples of taken-for-granted beliefs in Western society are: doing things faster is better; there is such a thing as a perfect body (as portrayed by the fashion and film industries); the patriarchal world of empire, scarcity, isolation, competition and control results in improving companies' bottom line, budget, market position and other outcomes; technology is connectedness; progress is measured by wealth; there is not enough for everyone; outsourcing our lives to experts is advancement; and so forth.

Within the global world that we live in we are not only confronted with cultural and **societal ideas and beliefs** where we live, but also with the multiplicity of taken-for-granted ideas and beliefs that we are now invited into through technology and the media. We are bombarded with ideas and beliefs about what is good, acceptable, right, success, progress and development. It comes at us from all corners of the world, often leaving us confused and overwhelmed.

WHOM WE AUTHORISE TO SPEAK

People in positions of authority advocate taken-for-granted ideas and beliefs in ways that are certain and predictable, because they have a stake in their success and their effects on people. Examples of the strong advocates of such societal messages valuing what is important and what is not are doctors, teachers, leaders, psychologists, pastors, the media and parents.

Taken-for-granted ideas and beliefs support whoever is considered to have power and knowledge. In Western societies, institutions and individuals are supported by taken-for-granted ideas such as patriarchy (the privilege of the male voice as the norm), individualism (the individual is the primary unit of reality and the ultimate standard of value), consumerism (happiness can be purchased and measured by the number of possessions you have), ageism (stereotyping or discriminating against a person/group of people because of their age) and capitalism (trade and industry are controlled by private owners for profit), to name but a few. People and communities that benefit from such power constructions and relations sometimes colonise (take over or lay claim to) others (those who seem to have no power in this social construction), and speak and decide for them.

The power and knowledge present in these individuals, institutions and groups are hidden; they are masked in such a way that we never draw the conclusion that we could question these ideas or their messengers. We are therefore raised and socialised with these voices of authority telling us that "this is the way things are", never to be challenged or changed. For example, ideas and beliefs around success and achievement often show up in so many "I shoulds..." that people feel overwhelmed and doubtful about ever achieving what society has in mind for them. When I asked a group to reflect on whom they authorised to speak about their lives, someone answered: "Everybody else but me."

We also authorise those in power to speak about us and of us as experts in ways that say that they know and we do not. In this context we do not have a voice or a say because we are perceived as not having power. In our silence and complacency we authorise other people and groups to speak about who we are and what we can become and de-authorise our own knowledges and skills of living.

The Influence and Effects of the Taken-for-Granted

The relationship we have with the problem story in our lives is also a relationship with the taken-for-granted ideas and beliefs that have real effects on our world.

I Am the Problem

Problems try to hide themselves through the isolation they cause in the storyteller's life. They often make a person or community feel that they are the only one with this kind of problem and if others have this problem too, theirs is not as bad as my/our problem. Problem-saturated stories are invented as a form of social control by these taken-for-granted ideas and beliefs, because they measure us against the "normal" other, which never really exists.

Having accepted the I-am-the-problem belief we continuously engage in internal conversations in which we put ourselves down and trade to our culture the right to author our own stories, allowing experts and those in power to dictate how we tell and live the story of self. The things people then talk to themselves about, might be: "I do not fit in" and "What am I doing here?" Below are some of the messages that are constantly conveyed to individuals and communities by these societal ideas and beliefs in the Western world:

- You are not enough
- If you do not have money, you are nobody
- What you have is not enough
- If you are not educated at a particular school or in a particular way, you are nothing
- You have to be successful in a particular way to be accepted

People often ascribe the distressing and unjust results and effects of taken-for-granted ideas and beliefs to themselves. They think of themselves as failures, full of shortcomings or faults, and they are often implicitly encouraged to do this by those in positions of power. Those who are authorised to speak "over" others often leave the recipients feeling like docile bodies or subjects under surveillance, never measuring up, never quite getting it.

Western culture focuses strongly on the individual and the problem story, and these individualist lenses make us believe that we do not measure up. We end up saying: I am the problem.

THE GAZE

Michel Foucault described how those with power and knowledge of others give them "the gaze": "It is a normalizing gaze, a surveillance that makes it possible to qualify, to classify and to punish."[31] The idea of Santa Claus that some of us grew up with is an excellent example of the surveillance that starts to kick in from a young age. We were told that Santa Claus would know everything about us, whether we had been good or bad, even if nobody else knew, and this would have implications for our lives.

The gaze of those in power therefore affects what you wear, what you say and how, where you go and do not go, and so forth. With this gaze people feel they are under a constant surveillance that measures and weighs their actions to qualify them as fit to be on this earth as human beings.

SELF-SURVEILLANCE

These internalised conversations are possible because of a practice we call **internalised self-surveillance**.[32] Under the tyranny of self-surveillance, we are constantly thinking "I am thinking that you are thinking . . . about me or us". It is another way that socially constructed taken-for-granted beliefs and ideas provide a measurement whereby we can judge ourselves and others on how well we are doing in terms of society's requirements. We constantly compare ourselves to others, and this has huge implications for our identities, and our connection to the community and society.

We invest a lot of time and effort in what we think others are thinking as we are constantly engaging in relational and communal thinking. The way people dress when they attend a workshop, even when no dress code is indicated on the invitation, is an example of how the practice of self-surveillance shows up in our lives. As we look around the room we see that everybody is more or less wearing

---

31 Foucault, M 1977. *Discipline and Punish*, p. 184.

32 This section is greatly influenced and informed by Stephen Madigan's workshop at the 9th Narrative Therapeutic Conversations. For more ideas and thoughts see: http://therapeuticconversations. com

the same clothes. How did we all know to dress in a particular way, if no dress code was communicated? This is how we take up the practice of self-surveillance and reproduce it in all aspects of our lives.

Problems set you up to buy into self-surveillance, and then they blame you for having done it. Without an audience of judgement and surveillance, in the form of colleagues, our community, children, parents, relatives, God and neighbours, the problem story cannot survive. Surveillance is the delivery vehicle of judgement.

LABELLING

What is written in our problem stories was not written on its own. We do not come on our own to the stories of failure and deficiencies that we tell about ourselves; the stories we perform are culturally informed by taken-for-granted ideas. Labelling is one particularly pervasive way in which this is done.

As a society we have grown accustomed to talking about people – especially those who are different from us, by the labels we have given them. These thin descriptions of identity, or labels, then become the only way that a person/ community/organisation is seen. The effects and implications of talking in these totalising ways are formidable.

When a manager says, "You are a fragmented team," for example, he has a story about the-fragmented-team, a title that he has given it. He has woven different incidents together to form this meaning. He named the problem, but in such a way that the team is the problem. This is the trap of the languaging of our world: this way of speaking, in terms of a label, does not allow any movement. If we want to remove the problem, we have to remove the whole team. What happens next is that the team members take the label into their identities and start to talk about themselves in this way as well. Now they have internalised the story and are increasingly becoming the story they and the manager are telling about themselves.

Various taken-for-granted ideas and beliefs keep the story of a fragmented team in place, for example, there is no place for your humanity in the workplace; work is scarce and you have to compete with your team members to get to the top; speed is everything, so just get the work done.

There are various reasons why such stories are accepted. One reason might be that the manager has power, although he might be unaware of the power in the naming as well as in the way he is speaking. There is a whole body of knowledge about fragmented teams, and many books have been written to confirm their existence, characteristics and ways to fix them. These truths about fragmented teams, however, do not take into account the power of naming, the beliefs and ideas of the group, and the unique gifts and qualities of each individual team member's contribution to the team. The labelling has totalised the team and left it voiceless to question or challenge those notions that appear so real and true.

Labelling comes from a place where the rich knowledges and skills of living, the giftedness and uniqueness of the individual or group, are not accepted or valued. These ways of speaking are interested in speed and in fixing problems. However, when problems are "fixed" in the same paradigm in which they were created, nothing new can emerge. Labelling has no time to pause, to question, to explore, because it has no time for the rich descriptions of the skills and knowledges of living. Labelling has no interest in the effects of its speaking on people's lives. It lives in the certainty that all human beings are the same, that we can fix things fast and that we know what the end result will be.

LOSS OF IDENTITY AND ISOLATION FROM THE COMMUNITY

Michael White sometimes used torture as an analogy when he journeyed with survivors of abuse. He explained that the purposes of torture relate "to breaking down identity, to breaking down a sense of community and to isolating people from each other, to destroying self-respect and to demoralising, to depersonalising the world in people's experience of it."[33] Over the years I have indeed seen the broken down sense of identity and community, how people are isolated from one another, their self-respect being destroyed, the demoralising and depersonalising of the world in people's experience. These effects have, however, not come from the hands of abusers but stem from the powerful multiplicity of taken-for-granted ideas and beliefs of societies in the lives of people and communities.

When I facilitate groups, I often see the pain of isolation and loss of identity in the reflections of people's stories. So many participants whom I have journeyed with, especially in the initial conversation, numbly explain that they do not know what they like anymore (loss of identity) and cannot really think of who knows and cares for them (isolation from the community). These ideas are powerful, a form of exquisite torture that subtly colonises the territory of people's thoughts and longings and renders them crazy and out of pace with the rest of society. The invasion of these ideas and beliefs into our lives, identities and our connection to other human beings constantly chants: "You are the problem."

The message that you are the problem and are not good enough isolates you from the community as you feel judged and weighed down by the knowledge that you do not measure up. This drives people into silence and disconnects them from the very community that could support them as they live their lives. Within this de-humanising endeavour we disconnect ourselves from our own humanity and therefore also our connection to our neighbours. In this disconnect we have classified humanity into forms of "us" and "them" – forms that have isolated us from one another. A poignant example is the reflection of one of the black participants on the mines in South Africa: "I will now see white people as human beings and will no longer be afraid to engage with them."

Culturally we produce one another, as we can never be "outside" culture. Conversations that constantly compare you with the so-called norm or "other"

---

33 White, M. 1995. *Re-authoring Lives: Interviews and Essays*, p. 90.

and then rate, grade and weigh you accordingly, accomplish the ultimate; they eventually split people up and isolate them from one another.

GRIEF, DESPAIR AND DISCONNECTION

People get caught up in these ideas and expectations to the point where, in the overwhelming drive to please and impress others, they are sometimes disconnected from the things they really love and value.

The strong voice of these internalised taken-for-granted ideas and beliefs brings a kind of grief or sadness that reduces the possibilities for people to act, for this thinking negates experiences of human aliveness. We then experience further docility, invisibility and a reluctance to participate with our knowledges and expertise when it comes to writing the stories of who we are and what we can become.

Within the Narrative approach we are aware that taken-for-granted ideas and beliefs are powerful because they have survived over a long period of time and we know their strength is hidden, especially when shrouded in good intentions. When people question and challenge these ideas, they feel overwhelmed in their presence because these ideas often cannot be linked to a face or to a door at which you can lay a complaint. As we live with these powerful beliefs and ideas, our expectations can be lowered to the point of despair, about ever really changing our own life stories or those of our institutions. If we are overtaken and overwhelmed by the given world's taken-for-granted beliefs and ideas, there is no room for the imagination, for possibilities or for an alternative future.

The Narrative work cannot but be about social justice in a world filled with oppressive ideas and practices. The work wills and creates the place and space for voicing outrage at the presence and effects of injustice and oppression, as well as the enslavement, stuckness and trappedness that these ideas and beliefs produce. The Narrative approach is based on an ethic of protesting against the surveillance that culture has introduced, which limits and judges who we are and what we can become.

HOW TO LIVE THE LIFE

Narrative practitioners are co-journeyers who question, confront and challenge the harmful effects of the power, the taken-for-granted-ideas and beliefs, and the knowledge of those authorised to do so, in the stories of participants. We are always aware, in listening and being with people, that we have to ask the following questions: Whose voices are privileged in the telling? Which taken-for-granted-beliefs and ideas have a say in this narrative? How do the power and knowledge of society show up in the telling? Who is given the right to speak about this issue? Who is benefitting?

Narrative practitioners not only stand in protest against the limitations of societies' taken-for-granted ideas and beliefs, but also unpack and explore beliefs and ideas that speak of ways to live and think differently from what has been permissible. In this way, taken-for-granted ideas and beliefs do not have the final say as "truths", but can be unsettled and troubled by alternative ideas and beliefs.[34]

As We Speak

Not only are we as narrative practitioners reflecting and aware of how we listen, and whose voices are being privileged, we are also vigilant in terms of how we speak. The use of **externalising language** – language that separates the person and community from the problem – is a means for us to stand against the way in which taken-for-granted ideas and beliefs speak. Societal speaking constantly attempts to find the culprit and label him/her as the cause or the problem.

Externalising conversations have the following effects:[35]

- Externalising the problem counteracts the effects of labelling
- Externalising enables people to work together to defeat or resist problems
- It reduces guilt and blame
- It provides room for greater responsibility
- It makes more visible skills, abilities, gifts, interests, competencies and commitments
- It opens room for the development of the alternative story to emerge
- Collaboration and cooperation become possible.

Narrative practitioners do not talk to the person as the problem. Storytellers are always seen and talked to as separate from the problem. For example, when a storyteller says: "I am so unhappy in my work because...," the narrative practitioner responds: "When does the unhappiness show up in your work...". Rather than asking "Why do you think you are unhappy?", which sets the problem inside the person, we would ask questions that distance the problem from the person: "How long has the unhappiness been with you in your work?"

When we speak in ways that do not label or locate the problem back in the person, we are challenging the notion of the storyteller-as-problem, and standing with people in creating alternative stories of seeing and living with one another. The kinds of questions we use in the Narrative work help communities and individuals challenge and question those labels that are so easily thrown around.

---

34 In an article in which David Epston remembers Michael White and the work they shared, David comments on Michael's "sheer delight with those ideas that unsettled or troubled the taken for granted and allowed for ways to live and think otherwise than had been previously permissible or even conceivable, given that such ideas had gained the status of a 'truth'." Epston, D. Remembering Michael White. http://www.narrativeapproaches.com/White%20Memorial_files/epston%20remembers.pdf

35 Morgan, A 2000. *What Is Narrative Therapy?* p. 24.

CREATING THE SPACE

The ethical question in this process is who benefits when we allow these voices of society to be heard and grant them so much power? Whose voice matters and where does wisdom reside for us? These are all questions that the listener constantly bears in mind. We have to be conscious of the power we hold as listeners when storytellers share their vulnerability. As listeners we have the power to turn the gaze of the problem story back on itself when we center the storyteller and his/her knowledges in the conversation.

The invitation to emerge from the participation in docility is made intentionally in the way that storytellers are invited to move into a reflective space to share their knowledges, expertise and wisdom without being judged. As a result, we ask: How can we create the space, the invitation and the conditions that are respectful of the multiplicity of stories, meanings, ideas and beliefs that will open up, amplify and enlarge an alternative life? This space is possible whenever we

- invite participants to reflect and participate from their wisdom, gifts and knowledges
- co-construct learning and knowledge together, and emphasise that everything we need to learn is in the collective knowledge we will share
- acknowledge and value every person in the room as living an extraordinary life, and create a space where it is safe to participate, as together we learn what is relevant and appropriate at that moment
- bring questions that mine and show the rich descriptions of who the storytellers are, i.e., not the poor, single and thin descriptions of humanity currently sold by society
- create spaces for human connection that challenge the isolating effects of these taken-for-granted ideas and beliefs
- acknowledge and celebrate the multiplicity of stories, gifts, values, hopes, dreams and possibilities of human expressions.

The compassionate, gracious and non-judgemental presence of every narrative practitioner accepts human beings within the uniqueness of their stories and fosters possibilities for alternative journeys already underway. These possibilities go beyond the thin descriptions of these taken-for-granted beliefs and ideas, as exercised by authority figures, but rather speak of the possibilities of rich descriptions of life.

THE EFFECTS OF THE ALTERNATIVE WAY OF LIVING

Despite the powerful effects of these ideas, human beings are often engaged in courageous acts of contesting and resisting which affirm their human aliveness in the most intense way. They develop rather fantastic ways of coping and challenging these fixed ways of being.

The Narrative work acknowledges the struggle, multiple grief cries and lamentations voicing this political spirituality that births liberation and freedom.[36] At these intense points participants are able to see that the effects of these ideas are no longer overtaking them in their thirst for mutilation and docility. Participants can escape from the harmful effects of these ideas and beliefs and invite ways of being that are more enlivening. These enlivening moments include creative and imaginative shifts when the multiplicity of stories is thickened through

- the naming of stories
- the naming of the taken-for-granted beliefs and ideas, as well as those who are authorised to speak
- seeing the sad effects and influence of these ideas on all aspects of life, seeing the ebb and flow of these ideas and stories
- remembering the moments in time of events, incidents and stories that told a different story
- inviting a community to come alongside in the exploration of the preferred stories of one's life.

Various participants have recounted that when they realise they no longer have to be mutilated and trapped by these ideas and beliefs, they can stand up to them and open up to the possibility of living an alternative life that will bring them the gifts of breath, joy, hope, vitality, energy, aliveness and sometimes laughter.

The arrival and naming of an alternative preferred story is, however, not a destination or a fixed place that leaves the community/person in a state of eternal status quo. It is a shift in the direction of the story and in what informs that story. In addition, it is a shift from the isolation of a problem individual to a community of co-travellers who are now authorised to speak about and engage with the alternative preferred story.

Choosing to live into an alternative narrative about your life/company/organisation, is a luxurious act and a reaction against what society thinks is right and good and can never be ventured into alone. Choosing a community of co-travellers who stand with you as you refashion and reclaim your life from the harmful effects of these ideas is daring. To collectively have the final say about who we are and what we can become, is pure freedom. We celebrate how participants have resisted, showed up and challenged these systems, and in so doing are shifting the future narratives for themselves and their communities.

In the alternative story we are transforming a surveillance audience into a community of concern that connects through a no-advice and caring attitude and reclaims the space of grace and hospitality that invites the surveillance voices to take a walk. The community of concern is therefore an antidote to **strangers**, judgement and surveillance.

---

36 In this regard John Winslade (2009:337) comments on what Foucault calls "'political spirituality':
    ... the most intense point of a life, the point where its energy is concentrated, is where it comes
    against power, struggles with it, attempts to use its forces, and to evade its traps".

In the Narrative group work that I am privileged to host, I have found that when the community collectively names the taken-for-granted beliefs and ideas, participants are always amazed at the similarities in the ideas that inform their stories. The gaze on the beliefs and ideas then becomes a collective gaze, taking participants out of isolation and into community.[37] The community creates the space for an intense point of resistance and outrage, a collective grief cry and lament, a collective territory or space venturing into new directions. The political communal spirituality joins forces to lead to the living of the life in a different world, territory or space that is collectively created.

The Narrative work is an invitation to freedom and liberation, as participants often experience the movement from their stories of being trapped or stuck within a **dominant problem narrative** and beliefs and ideas, to being able to choose and live into an alternative narrative. The methodologies of freedom are invited in setting up the storyteller as a human being who is a storying, naming, languaging, interpreting, knowledgeable expert who stands in relationship to both the problem and the alternative preferred narrative with choice. In crafting a space for human beings to show up within these understandings, connectedness and intimacy are created that open up a new world where alternative narratives are welcomed, and where human beings are transformed into the movement of human becomings.

---

37 Foucault, M 1977. *Discipline and Punish*, p. 184.

CHAPTER FOUR

RE-DREAM OUR WORLD THROUGH ALTERNATIVE NARRATIVES

Narrative practices invite us to re-dream a life, world and future through alternative narratives as we live into a different direction beyond what we have taken for granted. We are also invited to re-communalise a world that is trapped in individualism and isolation, by allowing a community of co-journeyers to walk alongside us. Narrative work calls on us to re-gift our world by receiving and giving gifts abundantly, as we allow a community of co-journeyers to see and name what we are not always able to.

In the Narrative work we see human beings in relationship to an abundance and multiplicity of desires, gifts, skills, intentions, knowledges, dreams, commitments, visions and values. This leads us to value the journeys of human beings in their uniqueness and diversity, as they lead extraordinary and "exotic" lives.[38]

Because of the prominence of the taken-for-granted ideas and beliefs in society, these qualities of uniqueness and difference are often rendered normal, deemed human nature or nothing special in terms of what we experience as the domestication of our lives. The emphasis and intention in "exoticising the domestic"[39] are therefore political, because they are situated in a world that is so focused on sameness, predictability, universality and global trends. It is a world that is settled into keeping the mantra of "the way things are" alive and well, so that it can be said: "This is the given world for us all." In the face of this given world, with its sometimes sad and oppressive effects, human beings show up, stand up against and transform those systems and ideas that order them about as they lead extraordinary lives.

INVITATIONS INTO THE ALTERNATIVE NARRATIVE

Often, as storytellers richly describe the dominant problem stories, explore their influence and history, and name the taken-for-granted beliefs and ideas that inform them, opportunities and moments arise where evidence of the alternative narrative comes to the fore. In the preceding chapter we explored the role of

---

38 White, M 2004b. *Narrative Practice and Exotic Lives...*

39 White, M 2004b. *Narrative Practice and Exotic Lives...*

taken-for-granted beliefs and ideas, and the importance of unpacking these knowledges storytellers live by in the re-authoring of their stories. The intense points of facing these ideas and beliefs often open up a kind of liberation and the possibility of living into alternative narratives. The unpacking and thickening of the dominant problem narrative reveal hidden treasures which are the seeds of the alternative narrative, with sentences such as: "But there was this one time ..."or "My aunt used to say about me...". These moments are what Michael White calls **unique outcomes**[40] or **sparkling events**, as they speak of a different kind of story, different kinds of knowledges and skills of living – an alternative story.

In a recent coaching conversation, the participant referred to this moment as an epiphany. She was very anxious about a job interview as she had been out of the job market for two years. When she reconnected to her preferred stories of work, the history of how she came to this interview, her deep commitment to and valuing of the work, as well as the **community of workers** she had journeyed with before, her whole posture changed. She looked at her watch and said: "How long did this take? I am ready now; it is no longer about the questions they are going to ask me."

When we journey with the alternative narrative, which we assume is always present or on the way, we are exoticising domestic narratives such as those evident in that coaching conversation. The alternative narrative is therefore not a new story without evidence and substance; it might just be a thinly described story or a story that has been disregarded or has gone unnoticed in this world. Exoticising what participants think is nothing special, significant or even normal, it is another way of standing against the given world's ideas and beliefs which want to discount aliveness and see such narratives as unsustainable, temporary, the exception and pie-in-the-sky thinking, devoid of any depth.

After unearthing the seeds of the alternative story, participants are invited to state their position on the kind of relationship they would like to have with the story. We explore the richness of the story by asking curious questions to thicken it, and so that participants can be informed at the point of choice around the narrative. We explore the influence the story might have in the future. The beliefs and ideas that would support it and the people whom participants would like to authorise to speak in this story, as well as the community they want to celebrate and journey with, are named. By unpacking all these accounts "we come to know the history of alternative knowledges of life and practices of living. It is through this unpacking that we come to know how people's lives are linked to the lives of others around shared themes and values. It is through this unpacking that we can engage with the unexpected. This, I believe, can make all the difference."[41]

When we link our lives in our human connectedness and relatedness, we are documenting and exploring outcomes that have been outlawed, as we notice what is possible for the future – something which can indeed make all the difference.

---

40   White, M 1991. Deconstruction and Therapy, p. 29.

41   White, M 2001b. Narrative Practice ... See: http://www.psybc.com/pdfs/library/WHITE.pdf

THE PORTAL INTO HUMAN BECOMING

In Western society we place a high value on the success of the autonomous individual, the power of which is fuelled even more by a consumer culture that commercialises the self. The self has become a commodity, a form of goods that can be possessed and has to be sold to the world out there, by the way we dress and speak, by what we have, who we know, how and where we have been educated, and how our package of strengths and resources could add value to the company or organisation.

Yet, despite the infatuation with the self-made man/woman as a commodity to be sold, it remains a judging and dissatisfied world. In this world there is constant anxiety, as the individual always lacks the latest product or fad on the market, is always desperately searching for the latest self-help book that would take him or her to real success. Human beings in this understanding of the self become resources to be exploited: "These days we experience encouragement from every direction to take possession of ourselves, to engage in the internal farming of our lives through self-cultivation, and to take up internal mining enterprises that have us digging deep to get in touch with our personal resources, and to excavate these resources so that they might be brought to the surface, put into circulation and capitalized on."[42]

There is a longing and a looking for a hero; people are glorified and worshipped in a society that values individuals who are experts at mining practices and who, through complete possession of themselves, made it to the top on their own. Within this context, naming and journeying with the alternative narrative could so easily be co-opted as yet another way of being able to sell the self, to get ahead and claim that the self has just been immensely improved by a technique called Narrative therapy.

In the Narrative work, the self is not seen as the person you become more of as you throw away oppressive things within yourself, nor is it an onion that is peeled down to its centre where the true, real, singular and authentic self resides. Within this work, the self is constructed in different relationships, and therefore human beings are seen within a multiplicity of selves, a multiplicity of communities and a multiplicity of authenticities.[43]

Seeing ourselves as human becomings means that it is "always about becoming other than what we have been, rather than [to a] becoming more true to who we are."[44] When a participant chooses to live into and thicken an alternative story it is not seen as the final destination, an arrival or a homecoming. The journey of human becoming does not have an end destination where we can rest forever in the bliss of having arrived; instead, the journey is about the multiplicity of

---

42   White, M 2001b. Narrative Practice... See:_http://www.psybc.com/pdfs/library/WHITE.pdf

43   White, M 2004b. *Narrative Practice...* p. 89.

44   Winslade, J 2009. Tracing Lines of Flight, p. 343.

meaning making and about negotiating our identities in the multiplicity of stories that we call our lives. This journey is seen as a large-scale change in direction, one shift at a time, where a multiplicity of shifts will eventually change the landscape or the territory of the journey into human becoming and into a different future. Every shift is seen as small leaps into exotic and extraordinary stories of aliveness, stories that are no longer entangled in numbness and docility. It is a journey that is always on the way of making sense within the multiplicity of stories of one's life.

This journey of human becoming is not a journey that is or can be travelled alone.

FROM ISOLATION TO BELONGING AS A COMMUNITY COMES ALONGSIDE

As discussed in the preceding chapter, some of the important effects of the taken-for-granted ideas and beliefs are the experience of isolation from the community and the loss of identity. Problem stories isolate us and make us believe that the problem is inside us, that we are the only ones with this problem, that it cannot be overcome, and that we are so deep into this problem or the problem story is so deeply invested in us, that it is not worth trying to get out. All of these ideas put us at odds with society and sometimes with our own culture, as they become the conveyors of judgement, blame and shame. People then fall into silence and withdraw, in order to escape the judgement and shame which further isolate them.

When participants or communities name and choose to live into extraordinary alternative narratives, they receive no support from the societal structures, institutions and cultures that informed the problem story, since they are also beneficiaries of the perpetuation of these ideas. In addition, living into a preferred alternative narrative leads to a self that is constructed and re-constructed in relationships with family, neighbours, communities, teams, companies and nations, in new and sometimes challenging ways.

> *As I live into this alternative narrative and possibility it resituates the community around me, whether they are paying attention or not. But surely they are feeling and experiencing the difference in the dance, the melody and the rhythm. For some it is pure music and poetry and for others it announces the end of the reign of an ideology where everything familiar has been left behind.*[45]

The Narrative work is aware of the possibility of further isolation that can occur in the shift of thickening and fully living into the alternative story. Because the Narrative approach is built on the notions of our relatedness and connectedness to one another as human beings, it challenges the taken-for-granted ideas of individualism that believe we can and must undertake this journey, and could complete it, alone. We are therefore committed to not reproducing the very ideas and beliefs we are challenging. "Sending" participants into the world alone with a

---

45   These are my reflections on making sense of the journey of human becoming.

freshly named alternative narrative, without any support or a community to help them make sense of things, is indeed to reproduce the anxiety and isolation that accompany the effects of the world of taken-for-granted ideas and beliefs.

The Narrative practices see the self as constructed in relationships with others, and the alternative narrative cannot be sustained and enriched unless it is supported by a community. Participants and communities are invited to name a group of people who know their gifts/histories/values and skills and predict or expect them to choose and live into an alternative narrative. As participants name this group, they are "re-membering" their lives and stories out of isolation into community.[46] The re-authoring of the alternative story of a person/group's narrative is then renegotiated in this **preferred community** through many co-narrated conversations. This group of people (which includes things, animals, places or nature) we call a community of concern.

Within communities of concern the testaments of people's previously felt loneliness and isolation dissolve into social equality, solidarity, connectedness, belonging and togetherness within the community's interest in their wellbeing and becoming. The community of concern whispers the naming of the alternative narrative in our ears when we get caught up in the thin descriptions of our society's taken-for-granted beliefs and ideas about who we are. In the telling and re-telling of our stories to and within this community, the texts of our lives are invited to new meaning, as new interpretive lenses open up a space for hidden and long-forgotten narratives. They listen to us and breathe into our stories what we have forgotten or sometimes disregard. In this sacred listening and breathing, the community whispers of our becoming and of the extraordinarily exotic lives we are living. The thickening of the alternative story in this community provides constant movement, as new, previously unreached terrains are discovered. As one workshop participant said: 'The texts of your story and my story are now woven into the intertext of all our stories in a rich web of words."[47]

As the dominant problem narrative is left behind or inhabits a different space in the multiplicity of our stories, white lights illuminated by the community of concern explode like fireworks in the sky, opening up the possibility of the exotic. Aware of the ways in which we act together, the community is a creative, brilliant and transformative space as we all cross the thresholds of our own alternative narratives collectively. It becomes a place and space to speak and explore our thoughts and wishes, to be seen in a way that speaks of love and of being seen.

THE GIFTS OF THE COMMUNITY

The Narrative work has the following practices that further contribute to the thickening of people's identity conclusions.

Firstly, at the end of every session, the listener reflects and tells the storyteller

---

46   White, M 1997. *Narratives of Therapists' Lives.*

47   Heidi Moore shared this insight with us as a participant in the Introduction to Narrative Practices and Lens Workshop on 5 June 2012, in Washington, DC.

what s/he has learned from them, how the conversation/story has touched them, and where the conversation/story has taken them. This practice is also used in community-of-concern conversations, where participants are asked to write down the answers to these questions and give them to the storyteller to use as documents of their identity, in times when the ideas and beliefs of society are overwhelmingly loud and persistent.[48]

Since learning about Peter Block's Six Conversations That Matter,[49] one of which is about gifts, I have been calling such a reflection a gifts conversation. As we listen to the participant's story, we are touched, moved or struck by it, or we might even learn something from it. I think calling it a gift gives it even more power than the word "reflection". In the community of concern, members then say, "The gift I received from you in this conversation is ...". These gifts are contextual, specific and created in the conversation; they can never be reproduced in the same way since our stories are always on the move. I believe these gifts are folded into the rich fabric of our stories as we further shift the direction of our human becoming. When I refer to gifts in this book, I am referring to gifts that are birthed from conversations and constructed in these relationships, not gifts as the property or possession of a person.

Secondly, when the thin descriptions of identity are so entrenched that participants can no longer access alternative moments or events, a community chosen by the storyteller is often called to tell the stories that its members remember about the person. These stories tell of the skills, knowledges, gifts, hopes and dreams of the storyteller. These tellings are gifts to the person, as they open a door to remember these long-forgotten moments. They are like Gilles Deleuze's image of a fold: "As experiences are reflected upon, brought into conversation, unfolded and folded back on themselves... personal depth and richness of variation is constructed... Taking a moment from the outside of experience and folding it into oneself and then pursuing the line created by the fold in a direction that becomes a line of flight."[50]

In my understanding we are folding these unique experiences, moments, gifts, skills and dreams into the garments of our alternative stories with the witnessing and participation of a community, and as they are folded into the fabric of our alternative narratives, our narratives shift in preferred directions that re-author the world that we construct and co-construct.

WHAT THE ALTERNATIVE NARRATIVE IS NOT

The alternative narrative is not birthed in optimism or positiveness wherein listeners capture, pay attention to and applaud touchy-feely moments, or moments that society would value as successful, brave, courageous or ambitious.

---

48 Morgan, A 2000. *What is Narrative Therapy?* p. 86.

49 Block, P 2008. *Community* ... See chapters 11 and 12.

50 Winslade, J 2009. Tracing Lines of Flight, p. 341.

The storyteller remains the expert of his/her story, and therefore the expert of the moments and the uniqueness of events and meaning made that tell a different story. If the listener or the community of concern imposes what it thinks about a significant moment that needs applause and wonder, it is controlling and judging the story as it starts to have something in mind for the storyteller that most probably would reproduce the very taken-for-granted ideas and beliefs that have been challenged in the process. This can "contribute to a life lived thinly".[51]

As human beings start to experience themselves as authors and agents, a new constellation is created through the elevation of their subjugated knowledges, their relatedness to a community of concern, and the gifts, competencies and skills that they bring. In the process of inviting people into being agents and authors in writing preferred alternative narratives, storytellers move from consumers to citizens, therapists move from allies to co-journeyers, and all move from strangers to neighbours, and from human beings to human becomings.

The moment people dare to state the name and start to richly describe the alternative narrative, they take baby steps into a new direction of their preferred life, and create and open up a new world. As each person and community starts to fully and intentionally live into their rich, extraordinary and exotic lives, we are collectively re-dreaming what is possible for our world and its future.

---

51 White, M 2001a. *Narrative Practice...* See: http://www.psybc.com/pdfs/library/WHITE.pdf

PART III

HOW TO DO THE WORK

*Now that we understand why we do the work in a certain way
or what we are able to see as we do the work, we are ready to
explore how we do the work with individuals and communities.*

Part three describes the beautiful flowers that emerge from the roots of the fertile ground of the "why" we just explored. It will explain how these ideas and the philosophical approach turn into practices and processes that help to re-author the world we live in.

The Narrative processes are subject to the context of the conversation and the storyteller's and the listeners' co-construction of it; therefore, the flow of the processes documented in this section is a guideline to a conversation, not a template to follow slavishly.

Chapter five provides you with the tools that create the art of transformational conversations in which the Narrative work is set. The importance of how we listen, ask questions and document the work, will be explored.

Then a summary of the Narrative process and practices is given. The aim of chapter six is to provide a few pages that could serve as a guide to the possibility of the practices and processes that this work offers. This summary can further guide you to aspects of the work that interest you and will help you decide what is next for you in the discovery of this work.

Chapter seven explores a richer description of the Narrative process, with additional examples of questions to ask in conversations with individuals.

Processes and practices that create the space to shift the communal narrative are the focus of chapter eight.

CHAPTER FIVE

TRANSFORMATIONAL CONVERSATIONS

How we conduct the conversation needs to be in harmony with the philosophical ideas of the work. These ways of being are the caring hands that hold the work and invite the possibility of transformation.

In the Narrative work, every conversation has the potential to invite transformation in both the storyteller and the listener. These transformational spaces are created from the ground and roots of the work that invites everybody who participates, to see human beings and the world they are part of in ways that foster possibility out of the experience of being stuck. As participants in the process see the world and human beings anew, the quality and possibility of the conversation are opened within the multiplicity of stories, meaning, knowledges, histories, authenticities, gifts, dreams and communities.

Conversations in the Narrative work counter the isolation and loss of identity that often flow from the storyteller's and the community's taken-for-granted ideas and beliefs. For individuals and communities to decide to break the silence and end the isolation from problem stories, to enter a conversation, often takes a huge amount of courage. Transformational conversations support the movement from isolation to community, and from thin identity conclusions to rich descriptions of the knowledges and skills of living. The transformational space that carries this kind of conversation is given the significant responsibility of living the practices that honour this courage and shift the direction of these stories.

The art of connecting and engaging with the storyteller forms the basis of this transformational work, which is further supported by the way we listen, ask questions and document the co-creation of the preferred alternative future. These practices jointly invite participants to come as they are and to be surprised by the irresistible co-construction that the conversational space between the storyteller and the questioner/listener creates.

CREATING A TRANSFORMATIONAL SPACE

The first two practices in creating a transformational space are invitation and walking alongside; they support the listening and questioning that invite transformation to enter.

INVITATION

It is important to invite the storyteller into the conversational space by first deconstructing the power of the listener as the one who would know more about the storyteller's life. Often, when people enter the conversational space, they are used to experts telling them about their lives. So, the first part of the conversation is dedicated to situating what this conversational space is about and how it is different from spaces where the listener shows up as the expert and the storyteller becomes the object of the expert's advice. This can be done by telling the person what the assumptions of the Narrative work are:

- In this work you are seen as the expert of the multiplicity of stories that inform your life
- I am not here to judge your choices or your stories
- I am not here to tell you how you should live your life
- In this work the problem is the problem, not the person
- I am here to walk alongside you in the exploration of the stories you choose to bring into the conversation
- In this work you are seen as having a multiplicity of gifts, histories, commitments, values and dreams that inform your life.

You could also ask the storyteller if there is anything that s/he would like to know about you before you start the conversation. The storyteller is invited to ask any question that would support the construction of a conversation where there is the freedom to speak and say what would be meaningful to them.

WALKING ALONGSIDE

As active participants in the Narrative work, practitioners are intentional in co-constructing transformational spaces in a spirit of grace and respect, employing a non-judgemental attitude. Within this way of being, participants also do not have the experience that the listener

- wants to catch them out[52]
- is testing them
- is searching for something in particular
- wants the right answer
- knows, and the storyteller does not.

Narrative conversations are warm, sometimes filled with laughter, and could be described as two friends having a conversation about something that really matters.

---

52 Some approaches to conversations are constructed with questions and inquiries to point out inconsistencies in the thoughts, reasoning, actions and meaning making of the stories of people's lives. In these conversations storytellers often experience that the questions are crafted to set traps in which these inconsistencies become the focus of judgement and correction. In this understanding, the conversation and accompanying questions are aimed at catching people out.

TRANSFORMATIONAL LISTENING

The listener is always open to learn from the storyteller, and is open to being transformed in the conversation. Each conversation is regarded as deepening the other's understanding; in the Narrative approach understanding is always on its way, because we can never fully understand. In this exploration of understanding, transformational listening is reconstructing our worlds with each conversation.

If we engage in the practices below as listeners we are not moving to understanding but are imposing our beliefs, or even societal ideas, onto the storyteller. These practices prohibit curiosity because they are ready with the right answers. In addition, these ways of being assume that what was useful and helpful to one individual would also be helpful to others.

As listeners we are not in this conversation to give an answer or advice

- try to fix participants by
  - giving an answer or advice
    - "When I was in a similar situation, this is what I did…."
  - being helpful
    - "If you only follow these three steps your life will be so much better."
  - judging
    - "I think that was a bad choice you made."
- assume that we know what is being said and meant without asking
- applaud when we think something that is being said or an action was good or useful
    - "That was such a great thing you did when you applied for the scholarship."

Using these practices in the conversation would be re-creating the very ideas and beliefs that the Narrative work is challenging. For example, when we applaud storytellers for things they said or did, we encourage wonder, which discourages the intention to be curious. When we choose the stance of wonder, we assume that we know what is good and right for that person, which is a subtle form of judgement. When we foster wonder, it "invariably provides a fullstop to wider explorations, whereas curiosity brings with it opportunities for more extended conversations that contribute to an appreciation of complexity".[53]

Being aware of the stance we take as listeners, and what informs us as we are listening, creates the spaces we co-construct with storytellers.

As listeners, our role is to

- see the storyteller/community as the expert/author

---

[53]   White, M 2001b. Narrative Practice… See: http://www.psybc.com/pdfs/library/WHITE.pdf

- ask when we are not sure
- be curious
- be willing to be transformed in the conversation
- ask questions that we do not know the answer to
- be enchanted by the story
- think of the story in the past, present and future
- be passionately interested in what the storyteller is saying
- listen to the vocabulary of the conversation.[54]

Narrative work participants say that this way of listening is important as it opens up the mind and the imagination to new possibilities. In addition, participants comment on how simple it is to go deeper with their stories when they can speak freely, without judgement, in the conversational space. These practices of listening invite transformation out of isolation into connectedness and community, as the storyteller dares to say and is heard in speaking the unspeakable.

TRANSFORMATIONAL QUESTIONING

The second important vehicle for exploring the narratives of individuals and communities is the art of questioning. In the Narrative work we are concerned with what the questions do or do not do, the qualities of the questions, and what they produce and generate.

TO DO AND NOT TO DO

The intention of the transformational questioning in the Narrative process is to invite storytellers to tell their stories in a new and different way. To that end, narrative practitioners are constantly mindful of the effects of the questions asked.

Narrative practitioners don't ask questions that

- assume to know anything about the storyteller, without asking
- jump to conclusions
- judge participants
- know what is right for the other person
- belittle participants
- trick storytellers into answering in a particular way or giving a sought-after answer
- leave storytellers guessing or wondering what the questions are about
- address the person as the problem. For example,
  o Why do you think you are too much?
- invite storytellers to answer in ways that support the beliefs and ideas of society

---

54   Hancock, F & Epston, D 2008. The Craft and Art of Narrative Inquiry in Organisations, p. 493.

- fall back on the privilege of professional status ·
  - o In my professional opinion…
- invite answers that are ready, easy to access and waiting, like a take-away meal
- are about giving or retrieving information.

QUALITIES OF TRANSFORMATIONAL QUESTIONING

In the Narrative work transformational questioning,[55] which has the following qualities, guides the conversations in which storytellers and listeners engage:

- It is transparent, as storytellers are given the reasons, purpose and direction of the conversation
- It grows from the vocabulary of the conversation, that is, the language, text, ideas, stories, replies and questions
- It cannot be prepared in advance and is freshly constructed
- It flows from the reply and the context of the conversation
- It seeks the help, assistance and participation of the storyteller
- It respectfully appreciates the ideas of the storyteller
- It creates equal participation, where the questioner is led by the storyteller and the storyteller is led by the curiosity of the questioner
- It seizes the imagination
- It separates and detaches the person from the problem
- It explores the richness and multiplicity of stories
- It invites people to respond with willingness, excitement and readiness to participate
- It carries and conveys the fascination and curiosity of the questioner.

WHAT TRANSFORMATIONAL QUESTIONS GENERATE

Answers

Transformational questioning yields answers that

- matter deeply to participants
- are slow, like the speed of nature, which is contrary to the fast-track speed of modern culture
- are an outflow of the conversation.

---

55 This section is greatly informed by a discussion of the qualities and process of questioning in organisational work in The Craft and Art of Narrative Inquiry.

Continuing conversation

It generates continuing conversation from

- a desire from both the listener and storyteller to know more
- an expression of desire to continue with the conversation.

A unique and exotic vocabulary

Transformational questioning invites a story to be told and unpacked in a new and different language and vocabulary.

The unusual vocabulary shows up as we engage with the naming of the person's narrative and use it in the questions we ask. For example, we might ask: "What does the story of Profit and Production have in mind for the Excellent Service narrative that is so important for your company?" The participants cannot but pay attention to the question, because they have chosen the name of the story and therefore they recognise the naming vocabulary, as opposed to a language and way of speaking that are familiar to society.

Narrative practitioners use the unusual vocabulary of the storyteller. They ask questions that help the storyteller to name his/her story or to state the problem in a language that the storyteller uses and chooses. These kinds of questions might sound like this:

- *What would you call this story if you had to give a name to it, like the title of a movie or the chapter of a book?*
- *What do you think the story of Too Much has in mind for your life?*

We ask these kinds of questions because we believe that stories are created through language, therefore language is the medium for looking again at the story and re-writing it. When the story is named in the vocabulary of the storyteller, transforming questions focus on assisting the story to be re-told, so that it becomes more richly and thickly described.

Awakening

I will never forget a question from my first year in the Narrative practices course. Elmarie Kotzé asked me: "What are you teaching *Silent Servant*?" I still remember the reaction in my body, as though I had been thrown back in my chair. I gasped for breath. After that question I knew that nothing would ever be the same again, because I was awakened to the possibility of my own role and participation in the story. After the initial shock, I felt my breath and brain returning to my body, and a "revitalizing and enspiriting [of] all [my] senses" took place.[56] I was able, for the first time, to see myself as separate from the problem of *Silent Servant*, the story in which I was so immersed.

---

56   Hancock, F & Epston, D 2008. The Craft and Art of Narrative Inquiry in Organisations, p. 492.

Given that we make meaning of our world through language, questions have the potential to open up new worlds of possibility to us, as we are invited to think in unfamiliar ways. When we have named our story in experience-near language and are questioned in the language and naming we have just created, a new, magical world of meaning becomes available to us.

The quality of the wake-up questions takes the listener and storyteller down a rabbit hole of possibility where the imagination is unlocked and alternative realities can be explored, untainted by the fixed and given worlds where language and meaning are not allowed to move. Going down this rabbit hole is the invitation issued by every question born from the realm of curiosity. This curiosity can get our stories unstuck and open worlds where freedom, aliveness and movement into our human becoming are invited and celebrated.

Ethical ways of being

Narrative practitioners are aware that every question is intentional in its ethical stance. Questions are not innocent; they carry tremendous power and have enormous effects on human beings. As practitioners we are constantly questioning our questions, by asking: Why is it important for me to ask this question? Who benefits from this question? Whose voice is silenced by this question? Which ideas in society inform this question?

TRANSFORMATIONAL DOCUMENTATION

When the story has been told, it is the narrative practitioner's privilege to document what has been said and to return this documentation as a gift to the individual, community or organisation. The documentation serves as a retelling of the story and is open to be changed and challenged by the storyteller.

Transformational documentations stick to the unusual vocabulary and language of the storyteller. They are written in externalising language, which means that the person/community/organisation is spoken about as separate from the problem. In addition, some transformational questions are offered in this textured documentation. The documentation can take the form of a letter, a song, a poem, a film or a drama.

The documentation is written, sung or presented in the form of a story, where the storyteller is cast as the main actor along with the events and incidents that inform the story. The story is a rich description of the problem and alternative (with names chosen by the storyteller); the different beliefs and ideas that inform the story; how these stories influence the main character's life as well as the dreams, visions and hopes that flow from the preferred alternative narrative. Participants have reported that one such document is worth many sessions with narrative practitioners.

The particular way we engage, listen and ask questions grows from our ideas and assumptions about the world, about language, relationships, problems, possibilities and human beings that enable us to see, speak and be with one another anew and afresh.

The Narrative practices of creating space, listening, asking questions and producing documentations are the vehicles and invitations into a transformational journey of rich and textured descriptions of a life. These practices stand in resistance to a society that craves single and singular stories of the lives of individuals, communities and organisations. They also challenge a society that labels and names people and communities in a particular way. Transformational questions and listening invite participants to name their own experiences and stories. Chapter 13 more extensively explores the transformational nature of the Narrative work.

CHAPTER SIX

A WALK-THROUGH OF THE NARRATIVE PROCESS

*When there are eyes to see and a heart to connect, the
rhythm of the walk of the Narrative ideas in conversation is a
respectful walk, guided by the storyteller and the possibilities
of the practices and processes of the work.*

The intention of this chapter is to provide you with a summary of the most important aspects of the work that jointly inform, create and co-create conversations that transform. The Narrative process consists of various practices that participate in the conversation when they are called for. These practices flow from the roots and ground explored in the preceding section.

THE GROUND AND ROOTS OF THE WORK

THE NARRATIVE GROUND

- There is a multiplicity of narratives
- The storyteller is a knowledgeable expert of his/her story
- The language and the knowledges of the storyteller are central in the conversation
- The conversation thickly describes a life so often talked about as a singular or thin story
- Human beings are knowledgeable and skilful in the art of living and are supported by gifts, commitments, values, dreams and hopes
- Human beings are connected to nature, things, places and people who have been witnesses to their lives
- Answering the invitation to authorship opens the possibility to live into an alternative narrative.

THE NARRATIVE ROOTS

- The narrative is central in the work
- The problem is the problem, not the person, organisation or community
- The relationship we have with the dominant problem narrative is the problem
- Taken-for-granted ideas and beliefs inform our narratives and have real effects on what is possible in living life
- People whom society values as experts and authorities are often advocates for the taken-for-granted ideas and beliefs and what is possible in people's lives

- Distancing or separating from the problem narrative opens up the possibility to choose again
- The alternative narrative is always present or on its way
- A community of concern, rituals and celebrations and **documents of identity** are ways to thicken the alternative story.[57]

THE RELATIONSHIP THAT CARRIES THE WORK

The listener/facilitator in the conversation walks along or co-journeys with the storyteller in ways that flow from the roots and ground of the Narrative process.

- The intent of the conversation is to co-create an alternative future *with* participants, not *for* them
- Together, the storyteller and listener take responsibility for the conversation
- The storyteller and listener construct knowledge together
- The text and vocabulary of the conversation inform the questions.

A WALK THROUGH THE NARRATIVE PROCESS

Keeping in mind the ground and roots from which the Narrative process and practices grow is of the utmost importance. Failure to do this means the methods used will be dead techniques and the process will be one without eyes that see or a heart that connects.

The storyteller, the listener and the conversation provide the text for the work. Therefore, the process rarely follows set steps, as you would find in a recipe for baking the perfect cake. The rhythm of the conversation can be compared to a walk in a big park with lots of routes and benches to sit on. When you decide to sit on the bench in a conversation, it is a place where the storyteller decides to pause. The flow of the Narrative process can be described as different pauses, moments to explore, thicken, challenge, unpack, re-write, re-author and see anew. To think that we can prescribe to co-journeyers when to sit, how long to sit, and which bench or path to choose, is unimaginable.

The following "map" gives you a sense of the possible pauses, with an example of a question that could be asked at a particular "bench". A multiplicity of questions can be asked at every pause. Chapters seven and eight explore more possible questions for each pause in the individual and communal conversations.

Conversations are never predictable and certain, but if they were, the Narrative process might unfold as described here.

---

57 Documents of identity are rich narratives and descriptions of the skills, gifts, knowledges and relationships of participants that can be presented in the form of letters, songs, certificates, notes, poems, art, photos, etc. These documents support and thicken the alternative narrative.

UNPACKING THE PROBLEM-SATURATED NARRATIVE

Let's imagine that the context is a person coming to a coaching conversation to reveal a problem, a stuckness or trappedness that is overwhelming. When the existing narrative limits, restrains and gives participants the experience that they are stuck, we call it the dominant problem narrative.

The intention of this part of the Narrative exploration is to thicken the problem-saturated story. When this story is richly described, it enables participants to choose again what kind of relationship they would like to have with the problem story.

Furthermore, this exploration often opens up the unique moments of difference that are indications of the alternative narrative's presence. These might be referred to as an exception – "there was this one time" – or you might see a person "light up" as they look or speak differently.

Ask the storyteller to tell the story by referring to incidents and events that are proof and evidence of the story:

- *Tell me about the incidents and events that have led you to come here to talk to me.*

Ask the storyteller to name the story in their own language and words:

- *If you had to give the story that you have just told a name, like giving a title to a chapter or a book that you are the author of, what would you call this story?*

Let's imagine the name of the story is *Too Busy.*

Explore the taken-for-granted beliefs and ideas that inform this story:

- *What are the ideas and beliefs that you have heard that "they say" inform the story of Too Busy?*

- *Who are the "they" who say these things that are prominent in your life?*

Influence of the problem story:

- *How has the story of Too Busy influenced the way you see yourself, your work, your relationships, your god, your family, etc.?* (The list is endless; whatever you heard that is important for this person in the conversation can be explored in this question.)

History of the problem story

- *Ask the storyteller to draw a timeline, covering a period of their own choice, and indicate two things:*

> o *The frequency of the story of Too Busy showing up in your life*
>
> o *The intensity of Too Busy showing up. When was Too Busy the strongest, and when was it the weakest or not present at all?*

Statement of position

- *What is your **statement of position** on the kind of relationship you would like to have with Too Busy? Do you think that what Too Busy has in mind for your life is where you want to be heading?*

Ritual

- *What is the kind of ritual you want to engage with, given the position you have taken on Too Busy's presence and influence in your life?*

At this point the story can go in different directions. If a person chooses to stay in the same kind of relationship they currently have with the problem story, further explorations would be made around that. If a person chooses to have a different kind of relationship with the problem story, that will be the exploration. If the choice of the storyteller is to live into an alternative narrative, that is the direction to take in the conversation. The client is the expert and is always consulted around what would be a meaningful direction for them to go in.

THICKENING THE ALTERNATIVE NARRATIVE

Throughout the unpacking of the problem-saturated story, listeners look for moments in time (past or present) where exceptions to the dominant problem narrative occurred; these are the seeds for the alternative narrative. Again, this would be the way the conversation would unfold if stories were predictable and unfolded in these steps:

Ask the storyteller to tell the stories referring to incidents and events that are proof and evidence of a different kind of story than the dominant problem narrative they have named:

- *Tell me about the incidents and events where Too Busy did not have all the say in your life.*

Ask the storyteller to name the story in their own language and words:

- *If you had to give this different story that you have just told a name, like giving a title to a chapter or a book that you are the author of, what would you call this story?*

Let's imagine the alternative story is called *Breath*.

Explore the beliefs, ideas, values, commitments, hopes and dreams that inform this story:

- *What are the beliefs and values that inform the story of Breath in your life?*

Influence of the alternative story:

- *If the story of Breath were to have more say in your life, how would it influence the way you see yourself, your work, your relationships, your god, your family, etc.?* (The list is endless; whatever you heard that is important for this person in the conversation can be explored in this question.)

History of the alternative story:

- *If you look back at the timeline you drew,*

  - *how frequently has the story of Breath been able to visit and have prominence in your life?*

  - *when was the story of Breath the strongest in your life?*

The witnesses to the alternative story:

- *Who (animals, things, place, nature, people) would not be surprised that you are talking about the story of Breath in this conversation?*

Statement of position:

- *What is your statement of position on the kind of relationship you would like to have with Breath? Do you think that what Breath has in mind for your life is where you want to be heading?*

Ritual:

- *What is the kind of ritual you want to engage with, given the position you have taken on the story's presence and influence in your life?*

We name the alternative narrative and we enrich or thicken this narrative by imagining how it will influence our lives in the future. We also explore what kinds of ideas and beliefs will support it. We construct this alternative narrative with a community that values the rich gifts and histories we bring to the world, and is seldom surprised that we have chosen this narrative. This alternative narrative can be supported by written documents, music, rituals and celebrations.

The next two chapters will focus on a richer description of the practices and processes as possibilities for the Narrative "walk" and the pauses of the conversation.

CHAPTER SEVEN

PUTTING THE NARRATIVE PROCESS TO WORK

As we walk through the landscape of people's stories, the Narrative practices and process provide rich possibilities for the conversation to move beyond the world as it is seen and known. The philosophical ideas that inform Narrative work bloom in practices and ways of being with people that transform both the storyteller and the listener.

This chapter provides a more detailed description of the Narrative process, using the metaphor of the universe, constellations and stars, to explain how we understand the weaving of the different elements of meaning into the stories of our lives. It shows many more questions to ask at every juncture in the process. The questions are, however, just examples of the Narrative work. In the conversations we have, the questions flow from the vocabulary and knowledges constructed in the conversation, and are therefore specific and local.

The Narrative process unfolds in its own way in the conversations and will rarely follow the steps and order presented here. Also, this chapter is not a complete representation of all kinds of possible questions that could be asked during every part of the process, as questions flow from the language and replies that arise during the conversation.[58]

CALLING OUT THE STARS IN THE CONSTELLATION

If we think of incidents in our lives as stars, the way we make meaning is by drawing connections between the separate stars, to eventually draw a constellation of meaning into being.

A constellation is a pattern of several stars that make a picture in the sky, as seen from Earth. In reality, the stars in these constellations have no real connection to one another and can be vast distances apart. As we look at these constellations two-dimensionally, they seem to form patterns that are easy for us to identify. These patterns are then named as objects, animals and/or people. An example in the Southern Hemisphere is the Southern Cross, and in the Northern Hemisphere we can see the Big Dipper.

In the Narrative approach we invite participants to plot the constellation of their story by talking about specific incidents, or stars, that make up their story. When

---

58 At the end of the book I provide a reading list with websites and books that will enable you to access other examples of questions and practices.

we look at these incidents, some appear in that moment to be more important than others. As we start to make meaning of the significance of a particular incident, we begin to see other incidents that speak of the same meaning and story. Because we constantly try to make meaning of these incidents or stars, we connect the kinds of incidents that support a particular meaning we have constructed over time. Once we have collected enough patterns to make up a constellation of meaning, we are ready to give a name to the constellation of a dominant story in our lives.

First, we focus on the problem story that is told and performed, also called the problem-saturated story. These stories often leave storytellers with the experience that they are trapped or stuck in the story. The Narrative process creates a conversational space for participants to be clear on the narrative and name the incidents that are important stars in the constellation they drew meaning from.

Questions for getting clear on the narrative:

- *What story are you currently telling about yourself?*
- *If you had to choose five significant incidents in this narrative, what would you choose?*
- *When you look up at the sky of your narrative, what are the moments where you drew certain conclusions about life?*
- *What are the threads that tie these stars/incidents together?*
- *Where or from what in this problem story do you take your identity?*
- *What is the story you have lived into so far?*
- *Given this constellation, what conclusions did you draw or what decisions did it lead to?*
- *What occurs in your life that confirms these conclusions?*

THIN AND THICK DESCRIPTIONS OF OUR STORIES

So often participants' constellations are thin descriptions or conclusions of a community or individual's story and identity that render them blind to the universe of possibilities of alternative stories in their becoming.

The dilemma we as interpreting human beings face, is that the story of some of the constellations of our lives appears to be so prominent and important that it becomes the only way we view our lives and identities. In the Narrative approach we call these constellations thin descriptions or conclusions, because they render us blind to the bigger story of our lives. People experience a trappedness, stuckness or incompleteness in the constellation of the meaning they have created, over time, in the relationships of their lives.

It is very important that the listener enable the storyteller to richly describe his/her life. So often people end up having extremely thin or impoverished descriptions or conclusions of their lives that sound like: "I am depressed", "I always talk too much", "Our team never knows what is going on" or "In our community it is everyone for himself."

NAMING THE CONSTELLATION
OF THE PROBLEM STORY

After describing the incidents that serve as evidence for the problem-saturated story, storytellers are invited to name the constellation of the problem story. As participants name the story, they are "transported back to Earth", where they can start to see the narrative from its rightful place. It is just a story that meaning was made from, it is not written or cast in stone. The story, however, has real effects on storytellers' lives.

Our stories are informed by the language we use to name the problem. One of the slogans in Narrative practice is that the *problem is the problem*, as opposed to the idea that the person is the problem. The practice of separating people's identities from the problem is known as **externalisation**.[59] Externalisation is not a method, technique or skill, but an attitude and a way of being with people where we talk differently through a shift in language. Because problems are constructed in language, it is also in language that we reconstruct the problem story in its rightful place in the universe of our lives. In creating distance from the dominant problem story through language, we make it a thing and capitalise the name of the story, for example, the *Silent Servant*, *Too Busy*, or *The Pussyfooting Team*.

The name of the problem story must be something the storytellers themselves choose, and for the rest of the conversation the problem will be referred to in this manner. A problem can be a metaphor, problems between people (blame, criticism, fighting); feelings (anger, worry, fear, guilt, depression) or cultural and societal practices (mother-blaming, racism, consumerism and so forth).[60]

- *Is there a name you would give this story/constellation?*
- *If you think of your life as a book, what would you call this chapter or story in the book of your life?*
- *If you struggle to think of words, is there an image or a song that comes to mind?*

After the problem has been given a name we can ask questions like:

- *What is Not Good Enough saying about you as a person?*
- *What is this team teaching Too Busy?*

The naming of the problem story opens up the possibility to begin making decisions about the problem's place in the universe of our lives.

---

59 White, M 1988/89. The Externalizing of the Problem...

60 Morgan, A 2000. *What is Narrative Therapy?* pp. 21–22.

THE WAY WE SPEAK ABOUT THE NARRATIVE:
EXTERNALISING/DISTANCING/SEPARATING CONVERSATIONS

In Narrative practice we work with the concept of externalising/distancing/ separating conversations. This is important in a society that has internalised problems and located them in the person/team/community or society. The internalisation of problems means that we talk about the person as the problem. The problem is privatised within their body. We label people and talk about them in such terms as the "inconsistent manager", "anorexic girl", "dysfunctional team" or "fragmented community".

Narrative practitioners are therefore attentive to how we speak, because we know that we are creating and constructing a world of meaning. In Narrative practice we speak in externalising/distancing/separating language. When the storyteller says, "I am such a worrier", for example, we respond by saying: "The Worry tries to work its way into your life through...." When we place the word "the" in front of the name of the problem, we situate it away from the person.

Externalising conversations establishes a context in which people experience themselves as separate from the problem and the problem-saturated descriptions that have sometimes become their identities. The person is no longer the problem, and the problem is no longer in the person. As people experience themselves as separate from the problem, their relationship to it shifts.

A thorough investigation and exploration richly describe the problem's tricks, tactics, way of operating, intentions, beliefs, ideas, plans, likes, dislikes, rules, purposes, desires, motives, techniques, dreams, allies, lies and tone of voice.[61]

Examples of questions that unpack the problem story include:

- *What words would you use to describe your current relationship with Too Busy?*
- *What has Too Busy talked you into believing about who you are?*
- *How has Too Busy convinced you that this is the only way to live your life?*
- *How does Too Busy try to get between you and your dreams?*
- *What effect has Too Busy had on your relationship with work and family?*
- *What are the tricks and tactics that Too Busy uses to remain in this prominent position in your life?*
- *What intentions and desires does Too Busy have for your life?*
- *What does Too Busy have in mind for you?*
- *Which allies does Too Busy draw on, to convince you that this is all there is to your life?*
- *What are the deceits and lies that Too Busy tricks you with?*[62]

---

61   Morgan, A 2000. *What is Narrative Therapy?* p. 25.

62   Morgan, A 2000. *What is Narrative Therapy?* pp. 20–25.

In the Narrative work we come alongside people to raise suspicion of the problem story, as we invite them to thicken the story so that room will be opened for the multiplicity of stories of lived experience.

THE TAKEN-FOR-GRANTED IDEAS OF SOCIETY INFORMING OUR STORIES

After we have richly described the problem narrative, we continue on the path of further separating from the problem story by exploring the taken-for-granted ideas and beliefs, as well as those we have authorised to speak about our stories.

The power of the constellation of our problem story is that it renders us blind and unable to see how taken-for-granted beliefs and ideas, as well as power, play into these stories. These ideas may seem innocent, but they are powerful and mostly hidden in sustaining the problem story as a kind of life force that can speak with so much authority in our lives.

In the Narrative approach we are interested in discovering, acknowledging and unpacking the beliefs and ideas of society that serve to assist the problem story. We could therefore ask the following questions:

- *What are some of the taken-for-granted ways of living and being that are assisting the life of the problem?*
- *How have you taken these taken-for-granted ideas and beliefs into your life and story?*
- *How did these ideas and beliefs develop?*
- *What are the ideas and beliefs in society which inform the story of this constellation?*
- *What are the background assumptions that allow this story to make sense?*[63]

Once we unpack the taken-for-granted beliefs and ideas, we further explore who informs and becomes the voice of these ideas.

WHOM DO WE AUTHORISE TO SPEAK?

Taken-for-granted ideas and beliefs are supported and asserted by people who hold positions of authority and power, such as teachers, parents, doctors, leaders and pastors. Those who are authorised to speak over others often leave them feeling like docile bodies or bodies under surveillance, never measuring up and never quite "getting it".

In our exploration we can ask the following questions:

- *Who are the people in society who enforce and advocate these ideas and beliefs?*

---

63   Morgan, A 2000. *What is Narrative Therapy?* p. 46.

- *Who is allowed to tell the story of this constellation?*
- *Who do you most often hear telling these kinds of stories?*
- *What is the narrative of the docility you have been living?*
- *How has the story of docility influenced you?*
- *Who has been supporting the story of docility?*
- *How is power masking itself in the constellation of this story?*

THE HISTORY OF THE PROBLEM STORY

Problem stories make us believe that they have always been there, that they own a big part of our lives and that they will always be there in this way. When we explore the history of the problem story on a timeline, or give it weight in an equation, we help storytellers to further separate their identities from the problem story. They can then clearly see the duration and intensity of the problem's presence over a long period of time. We could ask questions like the following:

- *When did the Worry first enter your life?*
- *How long has Too Much ruled your life?*
- *Was Difficult Community's reign over you equally strong over time?*
- *If you rated Distrust's influence over your team's history by giving it a mark on a ten-point scale, how much would it score right now?*
- *When did you first notice the problem?*
- *What do you remember before the problem entered your life?*
- *When would you say the problem was the strongest or the weakest?*[64]

In this telling and re-telling of our stories we come to understand the history of our lives as a much richer description than the problem story wants us to believe.

THE EFFECTS OF THE PROBLEM STORY

The next separation or distancing conversation from the problem story is exploring the influence of the problem on the storyteller. It is very important to take enough time to richly describe these effects, so that the storytellers can have a detailed perspective on and description of the problem's effects on their lives.

Relative influence questioning elicits two descriptions: the influence the problem has had and is having on the life of the person and, by contrast, the influence the person has had and is exercising on the life of the problem.[65] These kinds of questions help people to understand the breadth and extent of the influence and effects of the problem story on their lives. They can also reveal the losses people experience, or uncover aspects of a person's life in which the problem story has no say at all.

---

64   Morgan, A 2000. *What is Narrative Therapy?* p. 34.

65   White, M & Epston, D 1990. *Narrative Means to Therapeutic Ends.*

As listeners we are interested in the relationships storytellers have with all of the role players in their lives. We would ask questions like:

- *How does the problem affect your relationship with*
  - *yourself*
  - *others*
  - *work*
  - *God*
  - *life beyond work*
  - *your dreams for the future.*
- *How far did the influence of the problem story reach?*

We also ask questions around the influence of the person on the problem:

- *What have you been teaching Too Busy?*
- *How was it possible that Too Busy had no entry point into your work?*
- *What made it possible that Too Busy could not completely quench the fire of your dreams for the future?*
- *What are the choices which you are now making for your life, teaching Too Busy?*

STATEMENT OF POSITION

After participants engage in the rich exploration, unpacking and description of the problem story, by separating from the story and its effects, follows a very important part of the process: questioning the storytellers about the kind of relationship they now want to have with the problem story. Although these questions are asked throughout the conversation, at this point storytellers are asked to take a stand or a position on the kind of relationship they want with the problem story.

The conversation has now reached a turning point. Accountability, commitment and responsibility are possible when people are enabled through questions to see and **spy on the problem story** and distance themselves from it.[66] The storytellers can decide what kind of relationship they now want to have with the problem-saturated story:

- *Is this the kind of story that you would want to continue living into, or not?*
- *Do you see the problem story and its influence as a good or a bad thing for you?*
- *If you decide to continue to live into this story, what do you think this story has in mind for you?*

The process of externalisation helps participants not only to separate from the problem story, but also to further explore the exceptions to the dominant problem

---

66 Spying on the problem story means that we are aware of the story, how it shows up, when it shows up, how it invites us to pay attention to it, and what kind of tactics it employs to make us believe it is the only story that is real or true.

story. The next part of the process is to explore how to thicken the alternative story that would be the preferred story the person wants to live into.

Exploring the Alternative Story

"There is a crack in everything and that's how the light gets in."
– Leonard Cohen[67]

We started out by exploring the constellation of the problem-saturated or dominant story and gave the constellation a name. We then discovered the tricks and lies of the problem, the history and the influence of the problem story. In addition, we exposed the different taken-for-granted ideas and beliefs that keep the constellation of the problem story alive and authorise the problem to speak into our lives. These externalising conversations aim to separate people's identities from the problem story so that they can start experiencing themselves as authors and agents of their own universe of life stories. As authors and agents, participants are now invited to take up the storytelling rights of their own life stories through the re-authoring of the marginalised alternative story.

In the Narrative approach we assume that through the cracks in the problem story the light of the alternative story will start to shine through in the conversation: an alternative story that we believe is already present, but might just be hidden. Thickening this story of light is what this section focuses on.

The beginning question:

* *What are those moments, those stars resting dimly, waiting to be seen, that showed that you knew a different story was possible for your life?*

Alternative Stories Starting Out as Unique Outcomes or Accounts

The problem story always renders people blind to the sparkling moments or unique outcomes when and where the dominant story did not have all the say over the person or community's identity. We therefore start asking questions about these times and events, with respectful appreciation and curiosity.

In the Narrative approach the assumption is that within the story (even the problem story) lies the alternative future, and within the universe of stories of a person's life, there are always hidden stories and exceptions. These question and challenge the current dominant constellation of the problem story. Within the externalising process, the assumption is that these stars will show up in the conversation. When they do, those who are listeners are very curious about the existence and place of these incidents, actions or beliefs within the person's larger life story. The listener brings to the conversation the art of asking transformational questions that create the scaffolding to access these hidden and sometimes forgotten stories which feel like stars a million light years away.

---

67   See: http://www.youtube.com/watch?v=jykDA3cxeFs

These **counter-narratives** of hidden stories and exceptions open up the limitations of docility and complacency of people's lives. They allow participants to live into their human becoming as they re-tell how they have not been living into these limitations. After drawing out a full problem-saturated description, we ask the storytellers to remember occasions when they managed to get the upper hand over the problem or to think of occasions when they were able to deal with similar or related issues.

These exceptions to the constellation of the problem-saturated story are informed by clues that we get from spying on the problem through externalising conversations. We explore any account in this alternative direction with the same detail and thoroughness as we did with the constellation of the problem story. Every moment that looks different from the constellation of the problem story we call a unique outcome or a sparkling event. Unique outcomes are incidents in the past or present when people had influence over the problem and experienced themselves as free or distant from the problem story. These unique experiences form the pockets of light for an alternative preferred story and constellation.

The unique outcome may be a plan, action (sometimes just showing up for a conversation is an alternative future), feeling, statement, quality, desire, dream, thought, belief, ability or commitment.[68] Whenever the telling or re-telling of the unique outcome or sparkling event is witnessed, the person looks physically different: sometimes their eyes sparkle, and they pause as they enter the possibility and remembering of this story.

The following questions invite participants to notice actions and intentions that contradict the constellation of the dominant problem story:

- *Have there been times when you were able to rebel against the problem story? Did this bring you despair or pleasure? Why?*
- *Have there been times when you thought – even for a moment – that you might step out of the problem story?*
- *Have you been able to stop the problem from getting worse?*
- *What are the stories that are different from the dominant story of your life?*
- *What is the story that is hidden, that you do not give airtime to in your life?*[69]

As participants explore the unique outcomes, the process of thickening the **counter-files** of the alternative story begins.

THICKENING THE ALTERNATIVE STORY

When the storyteller has identified and acknowledged the unique experiences or outcomes, a thorough exploration is done to determine the identities of the person, apart from the influence of the problem story. The unique outcomes carry

---

68   Morgan, A 2000. *What is Narrative Therapy?* p. 53.

69   Morgan, A 2000. *What is Narrative Therapy?* pp. 57–58.

with them a wealth of gifts and skills for living that participants have sometimes not seen or acknowledged because of their fascination with the problem story. Because of the dominance of the problem story, these moments and events have often been forgotten, slipped out of their memory or been hidden. Narrative practitioners believe people have a multiplicity of skills, values, goals, gifts and knowledges that the problem-saturated story tends to make them forget.

Alternative stories that result from these unique outcomes therefore reflect both the richness of people's lives and their preferred ways of being known. The more detailed the investigation and exploration, the more thickly and richly described people's identities become.

Landscape of action and **landscape of identity** questions assist with the process of thickening and enriching the unique outcomes, and can be situated in the past, present and future.

Landscape of action questions

Landscape of action questions invite people to notice actions and intentions that contradict or deny the dominant problem story and to describe or expand on them in detail.[70]

Landscape of action questions ask: who, what and when? Here are some examples:

- *Where were you when this (unique account) event/action/plan/statement/ desire/commitment took place?*
- *When did the event/action/plan/statement/desire/commitment happen?*
- *What did you tell others about this event/action/plan/statement/commitment/ desire?*
- *What were the steps leading up to this event/action/plan/statement/ commitment/desire?*[71]

Landscape of identity questions

The person is then invited to reflect on the meaning of the events they have described. The landscape of identity questions ask about the why: What does this mean to you and why does this matter?

Given the answers to the landscape of action questions, what do these actions say about the person's desires, preferences, values, qualities, skills, abilities, intentions, plans and purposes? For example:

- *When you took this action, what did it say about what you wanted for your life?*
- *What are the values that made these actions possible?*

---

70   White, M 1991. *Deconstruction and Therapy*, pp. 30–31.

71   Morgan, A 2000. *What is Narrative Therapy?* pp. 60–61.

- *What did it take for you to be able to make this choice?*

- *When you took this step, what were you intending for your life?*

- *What do these actions say about your knowledges, skills, dreams and gifts?*[72]

The thorough exploration in this process enables the storyteller to gain clarity on the rich treasure chest of descriptions that speak of the alternative story.

Naming the Story

Naming the alternative story in the storyteller's own language is a very important step in further separating from the problem story and thickening the alternative story. Typical questions at this stage include:

- *What would you call this emerging story?*

- *When you talk about this unique outcome, would this be a good name for us to use for what you want more of, in the story of your life?*

- *What would you call the different kinds of stories in this constellation?*

Statement of Position

After the alternative story has been richly described and named, storytellers are asked to give a statement of their position on this story. It is very important to confirm that this alternative story articulates the preferred direction for their lives. Inviting participants to choose opens up the opportunity to again become agents of their own lives in the authoring of their stories. Questions such as these assist in further thickening the alternative story:

- *Is this alternative story the kind of story you would rather live into?*
- *Do you consider living into this alternative narrative to be to your advantage and to the disadvantage of the problem, or to the problem's advantage and to your disadvantage?*
- *Do you see the alternative story and its influence as a good or a bad thing for you?*
- *If you decide to continue to live into this story, what do you think this story has in mind for you?*

Authoring an Alternative Story

In this part of the Narrative process people are invited to start seeing themselves as authors, or at least as co-authors of their own stories, as they begin to move toward a greater sense of agency in their lives. The realisation that you are an agent or author is sometimes transformative in itself. The transformation from a passive/docile victim to an active agent/participant/author constitutes a powerful way of expanding and enriching the story.

---

72   Morgan, A 2000. *What is Narrative Therapy?* pp. 62–63.

Community of concern

In the alternative story, participants turn to a community of concern, i.e., the people chosen as supporters for the new preferred story. Because stories and identities are negotiated within communities, the re-writing and re-authoring of alternative stories can never be a solo endeavour. The people in the community of concern are often also the people whom the storyteller now authorises to speak about their identities, about who they are and who they are becoming.

Including a community of concern helps to continue the thickening and enriching of the alternative story. Questions to ask that would involve the community's voice include:

- *Who knows you so well that they would not be surprised that you are taking this step in writing an alternative story?*
- *Is there anyone you would like to tell about this new direction you are taking?*
- *Who would you guess would be most pleased to learn about these latest developments in your life?*
- *Who do you think would be most excited to learn of these new developments?*
- *Would you be willing to put them in the picture?*
- *To whom would you like to tell your different story?*
- *Of everyone who knows you, who are the people most likely to predict that you would find a way to choose this future?*[73]

Rituals of celebration

Rituals mark the celebration of significant steps and moments in the journey away from a problem story to an alternative preferred vision, version and living of life. The telling and performance of the alternative stories through rituals and celebrations can be transformative.

People most often experience the shift to the alternative story physically, as their bodies become documents of their newfound freedom from the problem-saturated story. The celebration and rituals could therefore be as simple as buying a new piece of clothing or changing your hairstyle.

Celebrations could also include people in your life who would support the new and preferred story. One example is to invite them to a meal and set the stage for the stories to be told on this occasion.

- *What would be an appropriate way for you to celebrate the alternative story and with whom would you like to celebrate it?*

---

73   Framework for a White/Epston-type interview by Sallyann Roth and David Epston. See: http://www.narrativeapproaches.com/narrative%20papers%20folder/white_interview.htm

REFLECTIONS

As part of the Narrative process the listener might be affected/touched/struck by the conversation and story. Together, listener and storyteller can reflect on some or all of the questions below:

- *What did the conversation do to you?*
- *Where did the conversation take you?*
- *What have you learned?*
- *What struck you in the conversation?*

As listeners ask these kinds of questions they are deconstructing their power by giving the storytellers the right to express what the conversations meant to them, without making any assumptions. Listeners further decentre their power by sharing what the conversations meant to them, and in these joint reflections, listeners and storytellers are both transformed and touched in the Narrative process.

The light of the alternative story now not only shines through the cracks of the storyteller's life, but also spills over into all the relationships the person is part of. For some this new authorship will bring life, while for others it will be scary, as the re-writing of one story is never solely an individualistic event, but a communal affair that has far-reaching implications for the worlds we live in and are now creating. The next chapter will explore the possibilities of practices and processes that are focused on shifting and rewriting the communal narrative.

CHAPTER EIGHT

RE-AUTHORING THE COMMUNAL NARRATIVE

*We are powerfully connected in a web of stories that open
up tremendous possibilities when communities join in writing
alternative narratives. It challenges the fascination with
individual transformation in our society when communities dare
to show up in the dance of communal transformation – a dance
that will take us to the common good for us all.*

In the Narrative work that I do, "communal" is used as an overarching term that can be replaced with "community", "team", "organisation", "group" or "nation". We can therefore speak about a community of workers, leaders, students, citizens and neighbours. The process and the questions that are presented in this chapter can be adapted for each context. As a result, the examples given apply to community in all its forms, as teams, neighbourhoods, organisations and nations.

As with our own life stories, the stories of communities are about getting stuck and trapped, and seeing the light through the cracks. Just as the Narrative process and principles were explained through the lens of the individual story in chapter seven, the aim of this chapter is to bring these practices into teams, communities and organisations, focusing on the different processes and questions that can facilitate the shift of the communal story.[74] Chapter 13 focuses on communal transformation.

NARRATIVE GROUP OR COMMUNAL WORK

Working with groups, teams and communities is a special form of Narrative work. In individual work, you have to invite a community of concern into the conversation, whereas in communal work the community of concern is already present, at work and participating.

When I work with groups of more than six, I divide them into small groups of three or four for all the conversations and exercises, so that all the stories can be told and all the voices in the room can be witnessed and heard. Participants are invited to form groups with people they know the least.[75] Numerous times, participants have reflected that they are surprised

---

74 David Denborough and Cheryl White have been doing groundbreaking work with traumatised communities across the world, and their work informs what is documented in this chapter. See *Collective Narrative Practice....*

75 Block, P 2008. *Community: The Structure of Belonging.*

- that the stories are so similar
- that it was possible to trust a stranger with their story so easily
- that the level of connection and intimacy was so much more in the groups with total strangers
- that the reflections of the gifts they received in the conversations were so much connected and in line with how they saw their own skills and knowledges of living.

These knowledges are then harvested by asking the small groups to reflect into the larger group.

The same Narrative principles for listening and asking questions that would be required in a one-on-one conversation apply to participants in these conversations. Guidelines at the beginning of a Narrative practices workshop create the context for the conversations as follows:[76]

You are allowed to

- be curious
- ask questions that you do not know the answer to, for example:

  Why does that matter to you?

- be willing to be transformed in the conversation.

You are not allowed to

- judge
- fix
- give advice
- try to be helpful
- applaud
- assume that you know what someone is talking about.

Participants usually remark on how freeing it is to spend time with a community, without the fear of being judged.

The same Narrative principles for listening and asking questions that would be required in a one-on-one conversation also apply to participants in these conversations.

INVITATION

In a society that judges, labels and knows about others so easily, the invitation to participate is very important.

---

76   These ideas are explained, with examples, in chapter five.

Narrative work facilitators are conscious of the power that is constructed between participants and themselves. This power is decentred through the invitation. For example, I intentionally explain that every participant has knowledges, skills and gifts in the art of living life, that are equally important. I continue the invitation by saying that I believe all we need to know and need to learn from one another is already in the room, and that it just requires our participation to be unlocked.

In all the processes and activities that are explored and documented in this chapter, the practices and values explained in the section above, will be the methodology to do the work and to be with one another.

The Narrative Process for Communities

The Narrative process is a dance that is tuned attentively to the co-construction of the conversation, never forcing its own way. The conversation can be as predictable as the steps here, but in the end, the community members are the experts in their story and determine where the dance will go and will take the participants. Inviting communities to be the expert requires that we create a space for relatedness, a willingness to not know (about and for them) and sufficient time.

Tell the Problem Story of the Community

The incidents that construct the story

- *What is the story that this community is telling about itself?*

Name the story

From now on, participants refer to the title of the story that has been named by speaking about it as the "Poor Community" story, the "Segregated" story, the "Everyone-for-themselves" story, and so forth.

Explore the effects/influence of the story

- *How is the story (name/title that was chosen) influencing how you think about self, your relationships, your work, your place as citizens in this country, and so forth?*

- *How are you as a community resisting this story that you have named?*

The history of the story

- *When was the first time you noticed that this is the story you are telling as a community?*

The meaning made of the story

- *Given the title of your community story, what are the meanings you have made of yourselves as a community?*

The relationship with the story and the story's relationship with us

- *How would you describe the influence you as a community have on the story, and the influence the story's relationship has on the community?*

The taken-for-granted ideas informing the story

- *What are the taken-for-granted ideas in your society and in this community that are keeping this story alive (for example, the idea of scarcity where there is not enough for everyone, consumerist ideas, patriarchy, colonialist notions and so forth)*

Power informing the story

- *Whom do you authorise to speak about you as a community?*

Take a position on the story

- *Is this still the story that you as a community would like to live into, or is there a different story that speaks more to the preferred identity of this community?*

EXPLORE THE ALTERNATIVE STORY

Name the story

- *What is the name you as a community would like to give to this alternative story that speaks of knowledges and gifts that are different from the problem story about this community?*

From now on, refer to the title of the alternative story that has been named by speaking about it as, for example, the "Gifted Community" story, the "Here Is Where You Want To Live" story, the "Community As Family" story and so forth.

Possible influence of the story

- *If you live into this new story as a community, how would this influence your relationship with yourself, your citizenship in this country and your possibilities as a community?*

The history of the story

- *Where does this emerging alternative story for you as a community come from?*

The meaning made of the story

- *How would you be speaking about yourself as a community if you lived into this alternative story?*

The relationship with the story and the story's relationship to you

- *What kind of relationship do you as a community have with this alternative story and how will the alternative story's relationship influence the community?*

The ideas and beliefs informing the story

- *What are some of the ideas and beliefs that would support the alternative story that the community wants to live into?*

Power informing the story

- *Who would this community authorise to speak about and of it?*

Statement of position

- *Given our exploration of the richness and possibility of the alternative story, is this the story that this community wants to live into?*

Thickening the alternative story through:

Community

- *Who in the larger society (or maybe another community) would not be surprised that this is the story your community wants to live into?*

Rituals

- *What are the things the community would like to let go of, and what would be a suitable ritual for saying good-bye to the problem story? (If saying good-bye is what the community prefers)*

Celebration

- *How would this community like to celebrate their alternative story in a way that would speak of this community's values?*

Communities of concern

- *What are the gifts that this community has and how would you like to share it with other communities?*

This process requires sufficient time for all the knowledges from the small groups to be harvested, so that the community can richly describe the problem and the alternative narratives.

THE STORY OF THE COMMUNITY

There are many more possible questions for exploring the dominant and alternative stories of the community. As an example, the story of my own neighbourhood in South Africa shows how meaning is made of a dominant problem-saturated story in a community and how the story of a community can be re-written.

EXPLORING THE DOMINANT PROBLEM STORY

The incidents and events that inform the story

I live in a predominantly white, middle-class community in La Montagne, Pretoria, South Africa.[77] The community used to speak quite frequently about the problem story of crime in our neighbourhood. The story of being victims within our society and country was built on the following incidents:

- There were hijackings in the driveways of our neighbourhood
- Residents were attacked in their homes and sometimes held at gunpoint
- Burglaries happened on a daily basis
- The crime rate was out of control
- Security companies did not respond in a timely manner
- Strangers visiting our neighbourhood or workers in the neighbourhood were attacked and robbed
- The police did not respond or come when called.

The community and neighbourhood made the following meaning as a result of these incidents:

- The police do not really care
- It is a case of every person for him/herself
- We are vulnerable
- If my walls are higher than my neighbour's, I will be safe
- We are victims of our country's inability to sort out the mess
- We do not have a say as Afrikaners, because our people were the perpetrators of apartheid.

Questions that help to unpack the problem story of the community

The following questions could be asked to help communities explore the incidents that are made meaning of in the telling of their problem story:

---

77   The information and insider knowledges about the journey of the La Montagne/Murrayfield/Val de Grace Community Patrol Association (LMMCPA) were provided in an interview with one of the founding members, Yolandé Giliomee. See: http://lmmcpf.info/english.html

The incidents and events that inform the story:

- *What are the incidents that the community is referring to in the telling?*
- *What do you speak to and about when you are together as a community?*
- *What is the problem story that you hold about this community?*
- *What limits the conversation for your community?*
- *What is the dominant story the community is telling about itself?*
- *What is the narrative you hold about your community?*

Naming the dominant story

The problem story of the La Montagne community was called *Unsafe at Home*.

- *Is there a name that you would give this story?*

Exploring the taken-for-granted ideas and beliefs

This round of questions focuses on the exploration of the taken-for-granted ideas and power in society that keep the problem story of the community in place. The familiar problem stories that we so often hear about communities are stories of Racism, Sexism, Homelessness, Youth at risk, Economic progress/development and the Poor.

Here are some of the ideas and beliefs that informed the story of the La Montagne community in the *Unsafe at Home* narrative:

- It's everybody for him/herself
- Nobody in the community really cares
- Something really tragic needs to happen before anything will change
- Because of apartheid, Afrikaners do not have a say in this country
- The government cannot keep us safe
- Nobody listens to the cries of Afrikaners
- Because Afrikaners were the perpetrators of apartheid, it is payback time and bad things will happen to them
- The police cannot keep us safe
- Because we are middle class, we are targets of crime.

Whom did we authorise to speak about the community?

- The Afrikaans media and newspapers were telling the community that as a country, South Africa will end up like Zimbabwe
- Julius Malema (leader of the youth league of the ANC) told white South African communities to go back to Europe

Questions to help us understand these ideas and beliefs in our societies

- *What ideas and beliefs in society inform this story of the community?*

- *What background assumptions allow this story to make sense?*

- *What are some of the taken-for-granted ways of living and being that are assisting the life of the problem in the community?*

- *Who is allowed to tell the story of the community?*

- *Whom do you most often hear telling this story about the community?*

- *When you as a community say that you do not know, to whom do you surrender the knowledges that you have?*

The history of the problem story

About eight years ago, people in La Montagne started to notice a gradual increase in the frequency and violence of theft in the community. Before the story of *Unsafe at Home* became dominant, people remembered when this area still had gravel roads and was part of a big farm. The story of *Unsafe at Home* reached a peak in 2008, when a group of neighbours came together to take action against this problem-saturated story.

The next round of questions helps us understand the history of the problem story:

- *When did you first notice this problem in the community?*
- *What do you remember before the problem entered the community?*
- *When would you say the problem was the strongest and when was it at its weakest?*
- *How is the community influencing the problem story?*

The influence and effects of the problem story

In the La Montagne community the effects of the problem story, *Unsafe at Home*, resulted in fear, anger, increased racism, more security, higher walls and greater isolation from one another. The community started losing hope for the future and for things ever really changing. In addition, the men were called out to assist in combating crime every single night in 2008.

Questions exploring these effects:

- *How has the problem story about this community influenced the relationship with self, others in the community, being a citizen of the country, those outside the community, the earth?*

- *How has the problem story influenced the community's relationship with the future?*

Statement of position

As community members started to talk to one another at church and at schools when they encountered one another, it became clear that *Unsafe At Home* was not the story the community wanted to be living with anymore. Some community members even decided to move to other, safer neighbourhoods, to show where they stood in terms of their position on this problem story.

The questions that can be asked to help the community take a stand in relation to the dominant story they are telling as a community, include:

- *Is this the kind of story the community would want to continue living into, or not?*

- *Do you see the problem story as a good or a bad thing for your community?*

- *Do you want your children to have the same conversations as you are having right now?*

EXPLORING THE ALTERNATIVE STORY

In La Montagne, Yolandé Giliomee and Liana Schönborn refused to be drawn into the problem story called *Unsafe At Home*. They started having conversations with a neighbouring Community Policing Forum (CPF) and convened a meeting to start the same forum in La Montagne. (Murrayfield and Val de Grace joined within a few months to form the La Montagne/Murrayfield/Val de Grace Community Patrol Association – LMMCPA.) After this meeting a group of neighbours walked from door to door to share the vision of the forum and to explain how it would work. In these conversations with neighbours an abundant community knowledged, gifted and able to live into an alternative story started to appear. As Yolandé and others listened to the extraordinary qualities of the gifts in the community, a group emerged that began speaking differently about La Montagne and the possibility of a neighbourhood where care and neighbourliness would become a way of being.

Unique outcomes and sparkling events

The moment the group from La Montagne invited the neighbouring CPF to teach them and listen to them was the moment the community started to rebel against the problem story of *Unsafe At Home*. Upon forming the CPF, the possibility of a neighbouring community rewriting the story about crime helped the people of La Montagne to begin imagining that it might also be possible in their community.

Questions to help the community recognise the not-yet-said and the not-yet-told stories that are already present, apart from the dominant story told by the community, include:

- *Has there ever been a time when the community was able to rebel against the problem story?*

- *Have there been times when the community thought – even for a moment – that they might step out of the problem story?*

- *What stories are different from the dominant story of the community?*

- *Have you managed to stop the problem from getting worse, as a community?*

The actions that the community took

A group of six families dared to gather and imagine an alternative future for the community of La Montagne. They acquired two-way radios to establish communication with their neighbours whenever they were in need. These families also called on the neighbouring CPF to come and assist whenever a crime was committed in La Montagne. Soon more community members bought two-way radios and started joining this action of taking responsibility for the safety of the neighbourhood.

The following questions could help the community to explore more fully the richness of the alternative story:

- *Where was the community when this (unique account) event/action/plan/ statement/desire/commitment took place?*

- *When did the event/action/plan/statement/desire/commitment happen?*

- *What did the community tell others about this event/action/plan/statement/ commitment/desire?*

- *What were the steps leading up to this event/action/plan/statement/ commitment/desire?*

What meaning was made?

The six families took the initiative in daring to imagine what it would feel like to be safe in their own homes. The values of care, support, cooperation, collaboration and walking the extra mile for one another, made this choice flow over into action. Initially the community intended for safety to return to the neighbourhood. The men in the community would go out and help whenever there was a call over the two-way radio, as the safety of each family became a collective responsibility. These actions spoke of collaboration: when we work and stand together, we all benefit.

Questions to guide the community's meaning-making of its actions include:

- *When the community took this action, what did it say about what the community wanted for the lives of its members?*

- *What values in this community made these actions possible?*

- *What did it take for the community to be able to make this choice?*

- *When the community took this step, what was it intending for its life as a community?*

- *What do these actions say about the knowledges, skills, abilities and gifts of the community?*

Naming the alternative story

The alternative narrative that was already on the way to presenting itself, was now called the *Caring Community*. This narrative spoke of the high walls coming down as it further revealed the possibility of again knowing one's neighbour. The community came out of isolation back into belonging, as the feeling and experience that everyone was alone and had to fend for themselves while feeling unsafe gave way to the alternative preferred narrative of a *Caring Community*. Although invested in the ideas of individualism, the *Caring Community* now realised that a group has a bigger impact than a single individual acting alone, and that talking as a collective provides a stronger voice than the single voice of the individual.

The community could then be invited to name the alternative story they were already living into and would further want to live into:

- *What would you call this _____ as a community?*
- *When you talk about _____, would this be a good name for us to use for what you want more of in the story of the community?*
- *What would you call these different kinds of stories?*

Statement of position

The *Caring Community* was indeed the alternative preferred narrative that the community chose, not as a new narrative but as a narrative that was already being lived by some members of the community.

The community could also be invited to consider their position on the possibility of the alternative story through the following questions:

- *Is this alternative story the kind of story the community would rather live into?*
- *Do you consider this to be to your advantage and to the disadvantage of the problem, or to the problem's advantage and to your disadvantage in respect of living into the alternative story as a community?*

Thickening the alternative story

In the alternative communal narrative, La Montagne was reconstructing the speaking with each other so that the community's gifts could be expressed, and collective agency could be revealed.

Beliefs and ideas

The beliefs and ideas that informed the alternative narrative of a *Caring Community* spoke of finding your voice and speaking out, of support for one another, and of standing up and saying: we have had enough of feeling unsafe in our own homes. The community invited the Wilgers CPF (a neighbouring community that was living the alternative narrative) to speak to them of this alternative identity of a

Caring Community, since Wilgers was a co-journeyer in establishing the possibility of La Montagne's new identity. In addition, the police, the church and school communities all became witnesses to the emergence of La Montagne's alternative narrative. Surrounding communities like Mamelodi (a black township close to La Montagne) started speaking about this *Caring Community*, where it was very difficult to commit a crime.

Questions to explore the ideas, beliefs and relationship with power that would enable the alternative story of the community to be lived into, include:

- *Who would you now invite to speak or authorise when it comes to the alternative narrative of this community?*

- *What are the beliefs and values that could speak into the alternative story?*

- *Who is allowed to tell the alternative story of this community?*

EXPLORING RICHER DESCRIPTIONS/CONCLUSIONS OF THE ALTERNATIVE STORY

The community no longer felt overwhelmed by the story of *Unsafe At Home*, as a sense of control returned in which people were no longer overpowered by helplessness and despair. The community now knew that they collaborated, constructed safety for one another, and opened up their lives and homes to an abundance of friends who were also their neighbours. The LMMCPA wanted the media to notice this remarkable re-writing and re-authoring of a community's narrative. The people who would not have been surprised that *Caring Community* was the alternative narrative that was being lived into, would be the police department, the older generation that had lived in the community for 30 years or more, the surrounding neighbourhoods that had been supportive along the way, as well as all the domestic and garden service workers working in La Montagne, who have now been trained to keep their eyes on the street in this community.

The police department has now been empowered by the community to do their work. La Montagne began caring for the local police department by celebrating each staff member's birthday, by giving meals on special occasions such as Easter and Christmas, and by giving gifts on Valentine's Day. The *Caring Community* invested its energy by caring for the local police department and has ever since been participating with the department in addressing crime in the neighbourhood. The police now often arrive at the scene of the crime before the security companies do.

In addition, the *Caring Community* has gone the extra mile not only with members of the community but also with total strangers who entered the neighbourhood. When they became victims of crime, they were cared for with the same level of support that would have been given to community members living in the neighbourhood.

Furthermore, the people who work in La Montagne have been trained to be the eyes and ears of the neighbourhood. Not only are they taking responsibility for the neighbourhood, but they are implementing similar ideas in their own communities. One of the communities in Mamelodi uses whistles instead of two-way radios when somebody suspects a crime is taking place. When the whistle is blown, the whole community supports the whistle blower. In addition, Yolandé and other La Montagne community members have been invited to speak in townships nearly 100 kilometres away, to tell the alternative story of this community so that they can learn from them.

In exploring richer and deeper descriptions of the alternative story, the *Caring Community* of La Montagne learned that the *Unsafe At Home* story no longer has any effect.

The following questions can enable a community to write and live into a rich description of the alternative story:

- *How might you as community stand up to the problem story when it pressures you to get caught up again, to refuse the requirements it imposes on you?*

- *How could your coming together here today as a community be considered a form of disobedience to the problem story?*

- *Given everything that the problem story has going for it, how did you as a community object to it pushing you around?*

- *What does this alternative story tell you about the community that you otherwise would not have known?*

- *Of all the people in the community, who might confirm this newly developing picture of the community? Who might have noticed it first? Who would support this new development in the community? Who would you most want to notice?*

- *Who would not be surprised that this alternative story is the one the community chose?*

- *Where do you think you will go next, now that you have embarked on this alternative story as a community?*

- *Is this a direction you see the community taking in the days/weeks/years to come?*

- *Is there anyone you would like to tell about the new direction you as a community are taking?*

- *Who do you think would be most pleased to learn about the latest developments in the life of the community?*

- *Who do you think would be most excited to learn about these new developments in the story of the community?*

- *Who would you be willing to put in the picture as a community?*

- *What do you think I appreciate about you as a community, when I hear how you have left the problem story behind and taken up the alternative story?*

- *Of all the people who have known this community over the years, who would be least surprised that you have been able to take this step?*

- *Of the people who knew this community, who would have been most likely to predict that you would find a way to choose this future?*

- *Given your expertise on the problem story, what have you learned about its practices that you might want to warn other communities about?*[78]

The alternative story could also be thickened and described more richly by the ritual, celebration and communities of concern practices used in the Narrative work.

Rituals

A question to thicken the alternative story through ritual is:

- *What things would the community like to let go of, and what would be a suitable ritual for saying good-bye to the problem story?*

Celebration

The *Caring Community* of the LMMCPA has had various celebrations in the form of camps, weekend barbeques and picnics, a patroller day to say thank-you to all the men and women on patrol, breakfast for all the CPA members over 60 years of age, a fun run and market day, year-end functions, women's days and yearly meetings where the whole community is invited with the leaders of the local police branch to connect with one another. La Montagne is joining hands not only with other middle-class neighbourhoods, but also with adjacent black and coloured neighbourhoods.

In the co-construction of a new preferred narrative of a community, it is very important that the alternative story be celebrated in ways that will again provide richer descriptions of this narrative, for example by asking:

- *How would this community like to celebrate its alternative story in a way that would speak of what the community values?*

Communities of concern

The *Caring Community* of the LMMCPA has now been a support to various other communities that have embarked on similar journeys. The local police department has been empowered through the *Caring Community's* involvement and through the way they took ownership of and responsibility for their neighbourhood. The community has also gathered the contact details of all the businesses in the neighbourhood, so that neighbours can support the local economy.

Furthermore, the older generation has once again begun to participate fully in community activities and they say they no longer feel so isolated. Their earlier

---

78 These questions have been adapted from the Framework for a White/Epston-type interview by Sallyann Roth and David Epston. See: http://www.narrativeapproaches.com/narrative%20papers%20 folder/white_interview.htm

despair has been replaced with a deep sense of caring, a sense of confidence that when you call on the short-wave radio, somebody will come and help.

The *Caring Community* has formed prayer groups, and therapeutic professionals have formed a support group. These professionals freely give their services to those who have been traumatised or have lost someone to death in the community. There is a caring group that provides meals and flowers to families who are going through tough times. A medical team of trained doctors and CPA members with a CPR certificate have already saved a few members in the area who suffered heart attacks, strokes or other injuries. There is also a team consisting of CPA members trained to respond to a break-in or to people being held at gunpoint. They all have bulletproof jackets and many of them carry a firearm. Another group worth mentioning is the camera workgroup. Ben Hechter, an electronic engineer, spent a year of work hours putting up cameras and developing a wireless network for the LMMCPA cameras. Many qualified members joined him (electricians, welders, other engineers, retired professionals), and now there is a fantastic camera network, supporting the LMMCPA as well as the police in finding criminals and bringing them to justice with the necessary evidence. The LMMCPA also has its own website designed and maintained by LMMCPA members in the Information Technology profession.

As the community members are experts in overcoming the problem story and living into an alternative story, they are now able to share their knowledges and expertise with other communities. In choosing a community to share their story with, they are able to become part of a larger community of knowledge around overcoming problem stories as communities, and finding support in living into an alternative future. This part of the process starts by asking the question:

- *What gifts does this community have, and how would you like to share them with other communities?*

A systematic exploration of the communal narrative leaves the community with a rich description of the possibilities, knowledges and gifts that inform the direction of the alternative narrative. It produces a shift in a communal narrative that is commonly believed in society to be impossible.

CONSTRUCTING THE COMMUNITY'S SOCIAL HISTORY

The Narrative approach values working from the place of identity with communities and participants. Starting with rich descriptions of the documents of a community's identity provides a platform from which the problem story can be explored.[79]

---

79 This section was inspired by ideas from the Therapeutic Conversation IX workshop in Vancouver and is based on the Narrative collaborative work of David Denborough and Cheryl White of the Dulwich Center in Australia. See: *Collective Narrative Practice...*

DOCUMENTS OF IDENTITY

During a community gathering (about 20 representatives of a community is considered sufficient), each participant is asked to write his/her answers to the following questions from their own individual and cultural story. The facilitators then read through all the documents and draft a joint document in which the different gifts of the community are highlighted. This document is then read back to the community.

These are the questions each participant in the community has to answer:

- *Give the name of a special skill, knowledge, practice, gift or value that gets you or your family through hard times*
- *Tell a story about this skill, knowledge, practice or value*
- *Give the history of this skill, knowledge, practices or value*
- *Is this story linked in some way to collective traditions (familial/community) and/ or cultural traditions? Are there proverbs, sayings, stories, songs, images from your family, community and/or culture to which these skills and knowledges are linked?*

Once all the individual documents have been collected, the Narrative facilitator records the gifts, skills and competencies of the community, and co-constructs a title for the document of identity with the community's input and participation. These collective representations form the foundation for a collective identity from which other conversations with the community can take place. In some communities – especially those that have gone through traumatic events – it is important to co-create a safe place for identity to be told, before dealing with problem stories.

CONSTRUCTING THE SOCIAL HISTORY OF A COMMUNITY

The community comes together in conversation, and by exploring what they love and what comes to them easily as a community, members are asked to collaboratively find a metaphor that would explain what they are about, as a community. The first question to explore with the community brings back considerations of reflections, stories and memories that light up people's faces and help them access these metaphors:

- *What do we all love, and why?*

Examples of metaphors used in constructing a community's social history include kites, trees and teams. These metaphors create a different way of talking and a different conversation in the community, that sparks rich descriptions and story development. After a metaphor has been negotiated with the community, the metaphor creates a safe space for the rich stories of identity to be told. The metaphor provides a frame for qualities such as the values, hopes, dreams and skills of the community, which can be explored and expressed in language that is known and familiar to them.

Next, the individual stories of the community members are explored. These stories are then woven into one document under recurring themes. The combined document is read back to the community and changed wherever the meaning does not speak to the experience of community members. The important questions to ask with regard to all these themes are:

What is the history of the community's...

- *hopes and dreams*
- *values*
- *important people and places*
- *things that anchor them*
- *memories*
- *stories*
- *cultural practices*
- *skills/competencies and gifts.*

Where does everything come together for you? (What anchors you as a community?)

- *Grounded in the histories (What is the history of this community?):*
- *People and places*
- *Memories, stories, songs, cultural practices.*

The individual histories are documented within the frame of the metaphor (tree, team, kite and river) chosen by the community. When they have all completed their histories (often on flip chart paper), community members have an opportunity to tell their story, and all the individual stories are put up next to one another on the wall. With all of the individual stories displayed on the wall, we ask:

- *What are the common themes of gifts/competencies and skills found in this community?*
- *As we look at the collective (all the trees/kites put together) what do we see when we look at this community?*

EXPLORING THE GIFTS OF THE COMMUNITY IN THE MIDST OF THE PROBLEM STORY

When community members have shared their stories with one another and the common threads and themes of the gifts of the community have been discussed and acknowledged, participants can reflect on the gifts, skills and competencies that are invited into the community, even in the midst of the problem story's dominance in their lives, through the following questions:

- *What are some of the strong winds/storms that you have faced as a community?*

- *What are the problems this community faces?*

- *What do you do when faced with strong winds?*

- *What are the gifts, skills, possibilities, competencies and special ways in which community members deal with storms and strong winds?*

In challenging times, communities can so easily be overcome by the thin descriptions of problem stories that render blind the rich knowledges and skills communities employ in overcoming challenges. Naming and documenting these gifts, skills and competencies, amidst difficult and challenging times, become the seedbed for enriching the alternative narratives of communities.

The alternative communal narrative of a family, neighbourhood, team or organisation holds the potential of putting the drop in society's ocean that will have a ripple effect in co-creating new ways of being citizens. Citizens who show up as participants and not mere consumers and docile bodies can challenge all the taken-for-granted ideas we have come to believe as "the way things are".

PART IV

NARRATIVE WORK IN THE ORGANISATIONAL WORLD

The Narrative work is now also dancing in the world of business and organisational life. It is a dance in which the steps and movements are still being figured out, and where we, at times, step on one another's toes. This dance is welcomed in a world of certainty, product, profit and competition, as communities of workers tell and re-tell their preferred stories of work and organisational life.

The philosophy and practices of the Narrative work also have powerful applications in the organisational world of leadership, consulting and coaching. The Narrative lens can be a useful way of seeing and working with a wide range of organisational issues – from leadership development to team building to diversity programmes. The issues and examples in this part of the book are a composite of the concerns and reflections of real-life clients and workshop participants who have co-constructed the knowledges for using Narrative ideas in work aimed at rewriting the stories of how individuals, teams and organisations function.

As background to this work, chapter nine provides an atypical lens in the form of the story of *Scarcity* and *Abundance* in the world of consultancy, coaching and leadership development. Chapter ten explores the possibilities of Narrative work in the realm of executive and management coaching. Chapter 11 offers a review of the taken-for-granted ideas supporting widespread leadership norms and practices, and an exploration of Narrative leadership as an alternative. Chapter 12 uses a story related to consulting with the Narrative approach in South Africa to illustrate the work of a Narrative consultant, and what is possible with the Narrative approach in organisational development consulting.

CHAPTER NINE

THE STORY OF *SCARCITY* AND *ABUNDANCE*

As narrative practitioners working in the corporate world we engage with a multiplicity of taken-for-granted ideas and beliefs that have certain expectations of us and the community of workers we engage with. Understanding, recognising and challenging the dominant story of Scarcity is an important step in journeying with people in the business world. We have a very important role to play in coming alongside the alternative stories of Abundance and the practices that are lived into daily by various communities of workers.

The story of *Scarcity* has a great influence in the business and economic world in the West, with its mantra "there is not enough!"[80] The alternative is the story of *Abundance*, and a shift to this narrative guides Narrative work for the world of leadership, consultancy and coaching.[81]

SHIFTING THE ECONOMICS

The economic understanding of scarcity is based on the assumption that we have unlimited wants and needs, and that there are limited or insufficient resources to satisfy these wants and needs. The highest cost of organising our lives and the economy around the belief of scarcity as our fundamental reality, is that we are persuaded and motivated to separate ourselves not only from our neighbours, but also from our souls.

Scarcity limits possibilities. It reduces the belief in possibilities. When we start to accept the notion that there is not enough, we proceed to circumscribe how we think and what we think is possible. It matters not whether materially we have

---

80 The idea of the story of *Scarcity* is influenced by Walter Brueggemann, The Liturgy of Abundance…, and Peter Block, *The Economics of Neighborliness.* See: http://www.abundantcommunity.com/home/posts/peter_block/parms/1/post/20110525_the_economics_of_neighborliness.html. Also see Olivia Saunders' *Shifting the Economics* (forthcoming). For a radio interview on this topic with Olivia and Peter, follow this link: http://www.blogtalkradio.com/robert_thompson/2012/03/05/robert-thompsons-thought-grenades

81 The first part of the chapter was written by Olivia Saunders, who teaches Economics at The College of The Bahamas. She is currently writing a book entitled *Shifting the Economics* and provided me with a summary for use in this chapter. She explains her understanding of the stories of *Scarcity* and *Abundance*, and then I reflect on the implications for the world of leadership, consultancy and coaching. Used by permission. © 2013 Olivia Saunders. All rights reserved.

plenty or little. Those with plenty never seem to have enough. They constantly seek to get as much as they can, while they can, so that others cannot get to it, because there is not enough for everyone. Those who have little, materially speaking, are constantly seeking to get whatever they can, whenever they can, because there is not enough.

The taken-for-granted assumption of scarcity sets certain behavioural patterns in motion: hoarding and competition employ winner-take-all strategies. These two behaviours underlie the price we pay for basing our systems on conditions of scarcity. Competition among people in their respective spheres of life for space, resources, education, healthcare, money or positions of power, is hailed as the best possible way for people to manifest their best self, or for them to achieve the best that life has to offer. Because there is not enough for everyone, it is acceptable to employ our time and talents to enhance our store of goodies, by taking away and depriving others of them. In a world of "not enough" we are able to sleep at night despite mass deprivation, because, after all, there is not enough to go around. Where scarcity is orthodox, we rationalise the inferiority of those who lose in the competition games and we can be satisfied that their deprivation is "their just reward" or we believe they are not smart enough or did not work hard enough.

This practised economics separates people. Scarcity thinking destroys community. The majority of people have not been able to benefit under the scarcity machineries. They live on a treadmill, running ever faster in order to stay in the same place.

The dominant scarcity economic construct of the day, as with others over time, is coercive. Humanity is subordinated to suit the economic system. The parent is transmuted into a worker and/or consumer, and is no longer a human being. The job, earning a wage and consuming are more valued than parenting. Parenting actually gets in the way! A scarcity-based economic system separates people from their identities and narrows their worth.

Rulership-cum-leadership, in whatever sphere, is deemed to be a scarce or limited trait, designated to be within the purview of a limited group or the entitlement of a small fraction of the human race. We see scarcity in governance structures, whether in business, government or religious organisations. These structures are generally pyramidal, so as to reflect the value of one group over another, to demonstrate that there is a top and a bottom. Those at the top hold the scarce, more valued positions in the organisation. If we review very carefully the governance arrangements practised around the world, it appears as if only a certain group of people have the capacity to govern or lead. This emerges even in some religious texts, which proclaim scarcity of leadership capabilities, where only those human beings of a specific sex can be gods or saviours, prophets or priests, or heads of households. In the political arena, only a certain group can have the authority of rulership/governance of countries. In some countries, access to the privilege of rulership is either by birth, by invitation or by initiation. In some cultures, rulership is further limited to persons of a particular race, tribe or ethnic group, religion, education or family background, or to those with material abundance. We see scarcity thinking at work in traditional business organisational structures.

In business there are assumptions about the gifts, talents and possibilities of what and how much those at the bottom of the pyramid can contribute to the organisation. The assumptions, which are undergirded by scarcity thinking, are based on the belief that those at the bottom cannot or will not move from where they presently are. Too often businesses pigeonhole people into certain roles: "You are a (fill in the blank)." Those at the top delimit the capabilities of those at the bottom, and we relate to them accordingly. Those at the bottom are not treated as well as those at the top. Because there are only a few positions at the top of the pyramid, those at the top do their utmost to protect their positions. It would not be smart to have those at the bottom reveal their gifts and talents. Scarcity thinking leads us to deny others their abundance. Scarcity thinking also leads us to deny our own abundance, as we imprison ourselves in our jobs and hold onto our positions because we believe that it is the only job we can function in.

At the other end of the scale is abundance. Abundance is more than what is physically present; it is more than we can see at any point in time. Ideas and imaginations are the forerunners of physical realisations. Abundance resides where impossibilities become possibilities. The innocuous seed is the potential of thousands of fruits. Abundance lies in constant renewing. Scarcity is in stasis, in a state of conserving and preserving in times when renewal is needed. Abundance incorporates the ebb and flow of life, the natural rhythm of life. This is the lesson from ecology. Life is dependent on cycles (circulation) and flows. The extent to which we hoard and privatise, and in other ways restrict the circulation and flow of resources within the natural environment, our colleagues, ourselves, is the extent to which we restrict abundance. A thought from each of 50 people circulating and flowing among them, produces more brilliance and splendour than the thoughts of a million people if they are stashed away and prohibited from sharing.

IMPLICATIONS FOR THE WORK AND WORLD OF BUSINESS

In the story of *Scarcity*, the list of scarce things is endless: time, food, water, money, potential, talent, ideas, business, market share, job opportunities and so on. As I write, I can immediately hear the voices shouting and asking: But don't you watch the news? What planet are you from? Don't you know that this is the world we live in, that there really is not enough?

The power of the story of *Scarcity* is that we have come to believe that this is the way things are; that this story is true; that there is not enough for everyone and that this is the way it will always be. The belief in this story has real effects on the lives of human beings:

- A complacency and docility that *scarcity* is the way things are and we cannot question this way of being and living
- A fear that we do not have enough and must therefore hoard and consume more

- An acceptance that some people will have and others won't
- A competition with others for whatever we perceive as scarce
- An anxiety to get to whatever we perceive as scarce, first
- A disconnection and isolation from our fellow human beings in our hoarding and race to be first.

In the corporate world, the story of *Scarcity* informs the following beliefs and ideas:

- Profit (for the shareholder)

  Because there is not enough, we have to pursue profit at the lowest possible cost, while we still can (the market is so unpredictable).

- Productivity

  Because there is not enough, we must push productivity to benefit from the market at all costs, and as soon as possible. The story of productivity then produces the following stories:

  o Efficiency: Our processes must be efficient, because production with the highest profit is the aim.
  o Speed: This efficiency requires speed that has no time for rest and pause.
  o A life committed to work only: The idea that employees do not have to see the sun come up or go down; they have to work long hours to show their commitment. This approach thrives on the accomplishment of the idea of productivity.
  o Performance: Because we cannot employ enough people (the story of profit), we must ensure that those we have are performing at their best, sometimes at a level and pace that are humanly impossible to sustain.
  o Employees are owned by the company: If the life of the employee is not dedicated to the story of profit and productivity, he or she may be threatened with losing their job.

- Competition

  Because there is not enough, we must compete for

  o market share
  o human potential and talent (supports the idea of head-hunting).

- Growth

  Because of the drive for profit and productivity, the idea of endless growth is sold as something that is actually achievable.

- Compliance

  Because of the urgency within industry to produce at a profit, compliance with policies and procedures ensures a workforce that never questions the way things are done.[82]

The narrative of *Scarcity* influences the story of Making a Living, because we have come to believe that complying with this story, with all its sub-stories, is the only way to survive in this world.

In addition, the story of *Scarcity* expects human beings to show up as machines, to produce and sometimes give their lives away to satisfy a story that can never be satisfied.

The narrative of *Scarcity* is authorised by people in powerful positions in the business world: shareholders, market analysts, leaders, CEOs, managers, supervisors, economists and the media.

The dominant problem-saturated story of *Scarcity*, however, does not have the final say, as a community of workers is challenging, resisting and living into alternative preferred ways of being. These stories may be thinly described and are often told as the exception, but communities of workers are daring to leave and challenge these thin identity conclusions and the isolation that the story of *Scarcity* has in mind for them.

The alternative preferred story might be called *Abundance* or Human Relatedness. What we will call this emerging narrative remains to be seen, but the alternative preferred narrative is being documented, told and re-told as we speak. The alternative narrative reflects a multiplicity of narratives, gifts, histories and possibilities, that speak of a world where there is more than enough for everyone.

---

82 These ideas and beliefs are informed by many conversations with my colleague, Pierre Blanc-Sahnoun, who works with the Narrative ideas in the corporate world in France. He calls these ideas the Big Five. See: www.lafabriquenarrative.org

CHAPTER TEN

NARRATIVE COACHING

*Narrative coaching creates a space for individuals to reconnect
the rich knowledges, values, passions and hopes in their
relationship to the story of work and work-communities, in which
they become the authors and co-authors in writing the story of
the companies they represent.*

The lens and practices applied in Narrative coaching, with particular focus on the organisational world, draw from the maps of the work described in part three.

THE CORPORATE COACHING WORLD

In the corporate world, the world over, coaching is a growing business. Companies hire coaches and direct employees toward coaching for the following reasons: They

- assist with employees' developmental plans
- bring employees on board in terms of the company's values and vision
- help high performers perform even better
- improve the leadership skills of managers and executives
- assist leaders who are seen to be struggling to keep up with the pace of the company
- assist leaders who struggle in relationships with team members and colleagues
- ensure buy-in to what the company has in mind for them
- as a last resort, see what can be done before disciplinary measures are taken against an employee who is not performing according to company standards.

The assistance of the coach is often set in the context of "fixing" and "developing" employees. In most cases, the aim is to ensure conformity according to an agenda informed predominantly by the production and profit concerns of the story of *Scarcity*.

These coaching initiatives might be ignited by a new change management process, a new leadership development venture, or a new values drive within the company. Generally, the focus is on getting employees and their leaders on board, getting them to buy into the company's direction and process, or developing employees for the next level of challenges they will be facing in new roles in the company.

The coaching journeys I have taken with executives managing in both the South African business world and international contexts form the composite illustrations in this chapter of how Narrative practices can be used in coaching corporate leaders. They can be coached in defining helpful ideas and values around leadership, how to relate with their teams, how to re-write the problem stories of their teams and their own lives, and how to be able to do these things amongst all of the pressures for profit and productivity. The rich histories, competencies, gifts and skills of these coachees have come to life within a community that supports their voices and helps them make sense of their world.

THE NARRATIVE COACHING PROCESS

The invitation to work with an executive in a coaching relationship often comes from the managing director or the Human Resource manager. I am briefed about the coachee and what is expected of me as the coach in this relationship.

Within my coaching practice, a whole day is set aside for conversations with the coachee, as well as team members in various capacities who work with the coachee. The coaching process starts off with a conversation with the coachee. During this conversation the coachee nominates colleagues, such as fellow executives and team members reporting to the executive/coachee, with whom I have conversations on the day. The conversations with these colleagues focus on the relationship and experiences of the leadership and the gifts, skills and competencies of the coachee. At the end of all these conversations, the common themes describing the kinds of relationships employees have with the coachee, as well as the gifts, competencies and skills, are all shared with the coachee. These first reflections also help to identify those important conversations which are needed (if any) with his/her peers.

It is important to journey with a coachee while honouring all the important work relationships he/she stands in. Working in isolation from the coachee's team and colleagues only further reinforces the powerful notion of individualism embedded in the corporate world. Coaching conducted separately from colleagues and teams reinforces the unrealistic expectation that leaders must take sole responsibility for issues and situations, and must, in solo flight, fix what needs to be fixed. When the coachee lives into an alternative narrative and the team is not included in the conversation around transformation, there is usually no support of or for the preferred alternative narrative. Sometimes there is even a longing on the part of subordinates and peers for things to return to the way they were. When the narrative of one person is transformed, it impacts on all the relationships and taken-for-granted ideas and beliefs that constitute the world as s/he knows it.

In the conversations with the coachee, we explore and name the story of the team s/he is leading. The coachee then has an opportunity to suggest experiences and conversations that will be conducted within the Narrative approach. These experiences can include team-building conversations, connecting conversations, diversity workshops and coaching workshops. As a Narrative coach, I come alongside and co-construct learning and connecting experiences with the coachee and his/her team in exploring and living into the preferred story of self, the team, work-communities or the company.

THE APPLICATION OF THE NARRATIVE IDEAS

Within the Narrative coaching practice, initial conversations focus on seeing participants outside of the problem stories, and exploring the name, influence and histories of the dominant problem stories which are all maps for the coaching journey. Understanding the particular taken-for-granted beliefs and ideas that inform the business context of which the coachee is part, is essential in the exploration. Journeying with participants in the re-writing and thickening of the alternative preferred narrative is also central to the Narrative coaching work.

The coachees with whom I have journeyed, have found the realisation that they are constructed by the stories they tell about themselves and the organisations they work for, both liberating and scary. This realisation is liberating in the sense that the story can be re-authored, and it is scary in the sense that coachees are participating in the construction of the relationship with the problem stories in both the telling and the silence.

The idea that the problem is the problem, and that the problem is not inside the coachee, is the doorway to a new way of living. This invitation is further extended to the teams the coachee is leading. As coachees become aware of the fixed and thin conclusions which these problem stories have in mind for their identity, a world of possibilities opens up, where richer and thicker descriptions become available. A question that could be asked in exploring a coachee's identity conclusions is:

• *If you no longer only took your identity from the stories of being a manager/ leader, what are the things we would be talking about?*

There are more identity-exploration questions in chapter seven.

In various conversations with coachees, I have experienced how the ability to see their lives through their rich histories, gifts, competencies and skills has been transformational. The transformation comes in the profound act of reclaiming rich descriptions of their identities. To be able to stand with rich descriptions of our identities within the multiplicity of our stories is especially relevant in a world where the language and single stories of profit, productivity and efficiency dominate.

Not only are coachees naming their own preferred stories within this world of profit and product, but they are creating conversations where their teams and work-communities can now name their preferred narratives. These teams and work-communities speak in ways where the problem is the problem, and where the rich identity conclusions of both the team and team members act as the lens through which they see the story of work. The re-writing of the work context and stories then flows over into celebrations around this important re-authoring.

A Story within a Context

In the corporate world, human beings are often referred to with thin and singular descriptions of the roles the company has given them, such as "employee", "manager" or "team leader". This way of speaking without names and identities creates a language in which employees are not human beings, but become tools and cogs in the big machine of profit and productivity. Furthermore, these names within defined roles are further described in terms of their efficiency and productivity: "inefficient leader", "low output team", "silo department", which are all ways to say that the speed and efficiency within this moneymaking machine are not up to standard.

The problem stories survive in a coachee's life because there are certain taken-for-granted ideas and beliefs in society, and particularly in the business world, that keep them in place. For example, the story of *Scarcity* informs the stories of profit, productivity, competition, growth and compliance.

In the Narrative coaching process, coachees come to understand that their stories are set in a particular context, and that the ideas and beliefs of that context predict and direct what is possible. For example, in South Africa the contexts might include the nation's story, the particular discourses driving the economics in the country (in the context of a specific company and ideas around productivity and profit and making a living). These taken-for-granted beliefs and ideas become part of the internalised conversations in which coachees often see themselves as the problem and feel judged by their peers and teams for not measuring up to the standards of, for example, being a good leader.

The power of these dominant problem stories is that they hide their surreptitious history, influence and impact on the lives of coachees. Sometimes the effects of these ideas and beliefs are the only indication of their presence, as coachees enter the coaching conversations with an experience of being overwhelmed by a numbness and a docility that flow over into a hopelessness, convinced that nothing will ever change.

Stories of Work

Within the story of *Scarcity*, coachees and teams' stories of work are often co-opted and overpowered by stories of profit, productivity, growth, competition and compliance.

Coachees are sometimes unable to remember why they are doing work in the way they are doing it. The following questions can be asked to assist coachees by providing rich descriptions of their preferred stories (counter-stories) of work that tap into their gifts, skills, values, beliefs, dreams and visions. You can begin the exploration by asking the coachee to choose something s/he values in their current work situation:

- *Tell a real and recent story that happened in your current job that illustrates "something that you value in your work"*
- *What is it in this story that is particularly precious to you?*
- *Are there any specific hopes, values, commitments, visions that relate to "something that you value in your work"?*
- *How did these hopes, values, commitments and visions appear in your life?*
- *What are some of the beliefs and ideas of your community (family, religion, culture...) that "something that you value in your work" connects you to?*
- *What would you name this story of work that you just told, if you had to give it a title?*[83]

The rich descriptions of the preferred stories of work that flow from this conversation become the springboard into other conversations that further thicken rich identity conclusions.

ETHICAL IMPLICATIONS OF THE WORK

Narrative practitioners are always aware of the powerful role they play within a context where employees, managers and the business world have something in mind for coachees. The ethical question "Who benefits?" is the guideline for the kind of relationship that is co-constructed and negotiated between the coachee and the coach.

Setting the stage for the coach and the coachee to be co-journeyers in an equal relationship is crucial in this process. The coach makes it clear that the coachee is not seen as a victim, as a person who is broken and needs to be mended, or as an object of the coach's development. The coachee is not in need of the narrative practitioner's fixing. In my Narrative coaching practice, the first conversation revolves around the coachee's meaning and understanding of coaching and development. From the start, coachees are treated and valued as the experts of their lives and stories; they are invited to explore the desired outcomes of the coaching sessions and to examine their own hopes and dreams against and in the developmental plan of the company.

These invitations to set the agenda for the journey are also invitations to take responsibility for the coaching process. The coachee's agenda might include understanding stories that s/he is stuck in, the influence and history of those stories, the taken-for-granted beliefs and ideas that inform those stories, and the possibility of a new and preferred story that stands outside the experience of being stuck in the problem story. As the coachee lives into an alternative preferred story for his/her life, s/he is invited to take back the storytelling rights in a context that often dictates how coachees should be in a particular role.

---

83 These questions have been adapted from handouts supplied at the workshop Pierre Blanc-Sahnoun and I presented at the Therapeutic Conversations X conference in Vancouver in May 2012: See: http://therapeuticconversations.com/tcxconference/tcx-handouts/

The answer to the question "Who benefits?" is that the coachee is the beneficiary of the conversations. How the coachee benefits is co-constructed in the co-journeying conversations. I never assume that the coachee is benefitting, or that I would know what that would mean or look like. "What would be meaningful for you to explore?" or "Is this conversation going in a direction that will be meaningful to you?" are ethical questions in the coaching journey. Questions around the company's ideals and intentions for the coachee are discussed, and often lead to decisions and conversations that are important for the coachee.

Although a number of coaching sessions are often submitted as part of a proposal to a company, the coachee is the expert in knowing when the coaching process has achieved the desired outcomes, as negotiated at the onset of the conversations.

The Coachee is not Alone

In a world informed by individualism and the story of *Scarcity*, coachees often find themselves isolated from their communities or friends as they wonder who they really are. In my work I am intentional in coming alongside the coachee as co-journeyer and inviting the voices of the preferred community and friends of the coachee into the coaching relationship.

In my Narrative coaching practice, coachees are not alone: rather, "we" stand on the shoulders of so many rich relationships that have informed the stories they hold as leaders or managers. The experience of senior executives and managers is frequently one where there is nobody to talk to, freely, without fear of being judged or fired for something they said. In this world of isolation and thin conclusions about identities, the Narrative coach walks alongside the coachee as a first entry and neighbour who breaks the isolation that is so often part of being an executive or senior manager. In addition, the coachee is seen as part of a community of people who support the preferred story of the coachee's life – a community that is invited into the conversation and into re-writing the preferred alternative story.

An Example of Practice

"I dread walking up the stairs to my office. What awaits me today? After I switch the computer on and the initial blow of the overwhelming contents of urgent e-mails has done its work, I take the stairs down to the canteen to fetch a cup of coffee, to help me take it all in. How will I survive?"

These were the words of John at the start of our coaching conversations.[84] It is a description and image of a life constructed in a corporate world that can sometimes be filled with much despair. The conversation unfolded life as is, John's given world, devoid of caution to express its bareness. Yet, underlying all of the numbness and docility there was a deep knowing that this can never be all there is...

---

84 The name of the employee has been changed to protect his privacy.

John is the financial director of a fast-growing multinational company in South Africa which is venturing into new business development in Africa. The fragility and vulnerability he expressed, and the desperation I heard in his opening words, cautioned me to tread lightly and graciously on this sacred ground of witnessing and co-journeying. It was an alert I almost always hear and respect early on in the coaching process.

As we explored a suitable title for the dominant problem story, John settled on the *Fireman* leadership story as an appropriate name. It was a very powerful story, one that coaxed John into always feeling responsible for putting out fires caused by people in the company, but also by outside factors. In addition, the *Fireman* story got John all worked up, because when he heard about problems too late, the story expected him to predict where possible fires might flare up. The story became too much work as John tried to bring about a controlled environment where improvements were made and maintained. Unlike the context of a real fire station, which has a team to address the threat of fires, the buck stopped with the *Fireman*. Through telling this story it became clear that John was the problem and saw himself as the problem.

Shortly after John and I spoke, he introduced me to some of his peers and team members. I engaged in conversations with them around their stories of his leadership and the gifts he brought to the various teams he was a member of. Everyone confirmed that the *Fireman* leadership narrative had its tentacles in their work relationships, but amidst all the anxiety of putting out fires, alternative stories of clarity, intelligence and an amazing gift with facts appeared.

As the coaching conversations unfolded during the next couple of weeks it became clear that the story of the *Fireman* was kindled in the context of the taken-for-granted ideas and beliefs of the business world, the particular values and beliefs of the company John represented, as well as the role of a financial director in a fast-growing company. The story of *Fireman* leadership can only exist in a world that has certain expectations of its workforce, such as engaging in restless productivity, being available 24/7, living with the constant awareness that you have to be grateful that you are able to make a living, that you have a job regardless of the cost to your own life and family, and working within the constant fear that if you do not go the extra mile you will be replaced.

The *Fireman* leadership narrative only made sense in the context of a blooming new business venture where things happened so fast that no one had time to reflect on the pace at which they were working, until their bodies began to protest. John always found himself in work situations where the business was experiencing tremendous growth, and he spent a huge amount of his time and energy putting systems and controls in place to manage risks in the growth of the business.

Lastly, the *Fireman* leadership story is mainly informed by the taken-for-granted ideas and beliefs that people in financial positions are often heartless slave-drivers who can only say "no"; that they are only interested in controlling everything, want to have the last word, and concentrate on things, not people.

As a result, working long hours under pressure with constant deadlines became John's way of being, the way things were. Through the years he was also rewarded in the business world for his *Fireman* leadership practices, as they brought him and the business the desired results. But these results came at a cost to his body and his sense of wellbeing, his family and his relationships with his team members and colleagues.

When John received 70–80 e-mails a day, 90 per cent consisted of problems that he needed to resolve. This left him overwhelmed, as the *Fireman* was constantly busy solving and handling other people's priorities and problems. Within this problem narrative, John ended up pre-judging colleagues and their abilities by how many fires they might cause and continue to fuel.

Finally, according to the *Fireman* story the buck stopped with John, therefore he took the responsibility for making a final decision on almost everything. He was accountable for it all as he protected and looked after the business. The *Fireman* narrative strained John's relationship with his team, as the task of anticipating and putting out fires was not the responsibility of the whole fire station or team, but rested squarely and solely on John's shoulders. This meant he was constantly reviewing his team's work.

Living into the story of the *Fireman* pulled John away from being strategic. He had difficulty anticipating events and could only think strategically about three out of ten times, which prevented him from seeing the bigger picture of his work.

The story of the *Fireman* also brought John's lack of work-life balance into view. The *Fireman* was on duty 24/7; John could not and was never allowed to switch off from work.

The most compelling evidence of the success of the *Fireman*'s narrative had been the strong internal audit rating within the company. So, even though John had a clear sense that this was no longer the narrative and leadership style he wanted to live into, the *Fireman* story was still close at hand, easy to access, and had been rewarded by the audit rating. The *Fireman* story remained the easy way out because it did not require any listening, he just had to do and he had to fix things that were wrong.

The business world and its expectations of John to be the *Fireman* became the seedbed for a new and alternative story which became the ground for a fresh future. He stopped doing what was expected of a *Fireman*, since he could no longer live this kind of life: the price was just too high. John could no longer be drugged by the claims of his current reality saying that "all was well". His body was protesting, as were his team and his family. The mandate to disengage from what had been known, fixed, given, and "the way it is" was no easy matter, as the old story would simply not let go of its protagonist.

Initially John felt too trapped and paralysed to access the energy needed to depart from the *Fireman* story. Then he found the courage and strength in the rich knowledges of what his family knew about him. John stated that he would rather live into a different kind of leadership narrative, which he called *Blue Sky* leader. This kind of leadership story values work-life balance. It also required him to coach his team members so that they were able to take responsibility for their own work. The *Blue Sky* leadership story enabled John to focus on more strategic business transactions, in order to ensure compliance from a much earlier stage. He described this leadership style story as an open style, where people are able to do their work and speak to him when there is a problem.

John started imagining different possibilities as he stepped boldly into the new world he was now creating and constructing. His alternative narrative authorised courage and summoned defiance. John authorised the voices of his family and friends to speak and tell the preferred story of who he was and could become. They were invited as the ultimate authority about the life and hopes of John as *Blue Sky* leader. The restoration of John's life served to generate energy and courage which enabled him to imagine and enact a future that the *Fireman* story had rendered null and void.

John created a space for his team to re-write their team narrative from *All Work No Play*, to an alternative narrative called *Together we Serve*. The team members got to know one another as human beings, listened to one another's stories, and saw the gifts and skills of their team in a new way. Because of the new relationship between John and his team, he began to take the risk of trusting his team members after showing them what to do. He now has weekly meetings with his team where he asks *Together we Serve* for their opinions. John has started building relationships with his team members through one-on-one conversations, and as a team they have had various celebrations of team members' birthdays. The qualities, gifts and skills of a loving father and convenor of a cycling team have enabled John to communicate his expectations to his team, as he now helps them to make decisions for the right reasons. He also helps them to say "no" when necessary, and he no longer tries to please people.

In addition, John, in the story of *Blue Sky* leader, is allowed to ask for help, and he has appointed new team members who lighten the load of the whole team. What's more, John has started to play golf again with his close friends, and even dared to leave his laptop at home as he went on a ten-day holiday to an area with limited cell phone reception.

I have seen the resistance against stories like the *Fireman* become a source of strength in pressing forward with re-writing other stories. In my own business, the anxious *Firewoman* shows up so quickly that I can be my own worst enemy and slave-driver. To constantly live into leadership stories of connection and being part of a team like *Blue Sky* emboldens me. It is a strong alternative narrative as I go forward, and a powerful new story for others I have journeyed with. For this insight we are grateful to John.

The re-writing and re-authoring of the preferred stories of one's life means standing at the intense point of challenging ideas and beliefs which, at the outset, present themselves as immovable and fixed. Daring to mount the stairs, move to the desk and open the awaiting e-mails without dread or fear of what awaits, speaks of liberation. It also speaks of being held in the alternative knowledges of the multiplicity of stories and relationships that ripple into re-authoring the world we are part of.

CHAPTER ELEVEN

NARRATIVE LEADERSHIP

*Within our work with leaders in the organisational world,
narrative practitioners are aware and pay attention to the
taken-for-granted-beliefs and ideas that inform and influence
what is possible for leaders. Narrative leadership practices invite
leaders to convene, to name and challenge problem-saturated
stories, and to invite alternative narratives into the conversation
as a participant with communities.*

The ceaseless focus on the meaning of the word "leadership", as well as the practices of leadership, has gifted us with a rich body of knowledge on the topic. This body of knowledge has become part of our language and conversations in the Western world, in such a way that we cannot imagine what it would be like not to talk and engage with the subject of leadership in the way we have done and are doing.

These taken-for-granted ideas and beliefs on leadership have, however, rendered us blind to the real effects and influence of this familiar story on all aspects of our lives. In addition, they hide the philosophical underpinnings that so strongly influence the conversation and present us with the world of leadership as we know it.

The Narrative approach grows from a different set of assumptions than the ground from which most current approaches to leadership grow. This chapter explains how taken-for-granted ideas and beliefs have indeed constructed a particular notion around leadership, and it unpacks the implications and meanings leadership has for the context, the leader and the follower. The unique Narrative lens and its practices is then shown as a possible alternative reconstruction of the ideas and beliefs of leadership which enables leaders to see and understand what informs their worlds.

Within this approach leaders are invited into a different relationship with those whom they journey with that opens the possibility of co-creating an alternative or counter-narrative in the context of communal and organisational work. This lens is respectful to the uniqueness of each individual, context and society, and utilises the abundance and multiplicity of narratives, gifts, possibilities and histories as a springboard and as evidence of the alternative future which is already on its way. So, this chapter is an invitation to rethink the role of leadership in which one of the goals and challenges is to co-construct and co-produce an alternative narrative that challenges the taken-for-granted ideas and stories we are currently engaging with. In this context, leadership can be seen as the act of initiating and co-creating a space for conversations about the alternative communal narrative that is already present or on its way.

THE INDUSTRY OF LEADERSHIP

Over the years, many descriptions, definitions, functions, actions and characteristics have flowed into the meaning-making of the idea of leadership. As the field of leadership development came into being in the organisational world, various workshops, books, assessments and models started to describe and train participants in all kinds of leadership approaches, including that of servant, tribal, strategic, visionary, transformational, situational and participatory leaders, to name but a few. The naming of the different leadership styles is usually determined through various assessments that reveal a leader's style according to certain categories.

Every new leadership description and style claims to have the most correct, most comprehensive or best idea yet. If we add consumerist notions to the mix of the leadership industry, the race is on for CEOs, executives and boards of directors to implement the latest "cutting edge" leadership model, as they compete to get on board first. In addition, the world of profit and production demands a leadership model that offers change and turnaround at lightning speed.

It becomes important for leaders to display their leadership knowledge by the number of leadership books they have read and the number of models they can cite. This display of leadership knowledge becomes a way of sizing themselves up against their peers in yet another race or competition to be the top dog. Being an expert on the bodies of knowledge in the leadership field, without necessarily practising the art, creates a hierarchy of leaders who tend to use exclusive language to describe their position and justify their actions.

Any new leadership model needs to be nicely packaged in easy steps, and must be supported and authorised by expert educational agencies and consultants, as well as the business press.[96] In addition it has to be verified by evidence-based research, where the "proof" of the success and effectiveness of the model lies in showing how much more money was made or how employee wellness rates have improved after implementing this new leadership style. These research projects seldom reveal what kind of methodology was used to determine how successful or effective the latest leadership style is, because if everybody is making money, who questions how the research was conducted? Thus, the real importance of the research is not what and how it measured, but that it happened.

The dilemma with some of these models is that they often make universal claims of the possibility of their successful implementation in every context and country at any given time. In this one-size-fits-all approach, the significance of context and meaning is played down.

Although we are still enchanted by the idea of leadership, there is growing dissatisfaction about leadership not delivering everything it promises. It appears

---

96 The practice of packaging and authorising maintains and sustains the scarcity of leadership, just like any other product.

that leaders do not always have the impact on organisations that has been assumed for so many years. What if leadership is a much more uncertain, multifaceted and incoherent phenomenon than we thought? If we dare to rethink, reconstruct and challenge these ideas and beliefs, with their accompanying emphases on the importance of leaders and leadership, we risk undermining the economically lucrative and enduring industry described above. But as long as the taken-for-granted beliefs and ideas of patriarchy and individualism still validate leadership, and the consumerist society funds its cause, it seems to be a die-hard phenomenon – for now.

What are the ground and philosophical underpinnings that keep the fascination and expectation of leaders in our society in place, well and alive? I invite you to read on.

The World That the Leadership Story Is Living and Leaning into

Our current notions and constructions of leadership did not fall from the sky. They are informed by the ideas and beliefs of the Western world. This world, according to Walter Brueggemann, has fallen into general uncertainty about, and disillusionment with, how things turned out.[97] The world that people are so disillusioned with is grounded in the taken-for-granted beliefs and ideas of patriarchy, individualism and consumerism. This disillusioned world longs for the objective truth claims, predictability, order, control, certainty and sameness that used to be the only real world. Often we hear people calling on leaders to take a strong stand, to put their foot down about something, to speak out more. These are all cries located within the context of disillusionment and uncertainty, cries expressing the hope that by leaders taking control and showing direction, some form of what was once known and familiar will return. So, the descriptions and explorations of the word "leadership" here are cast in a particular Western context, in which they make perfect sense to everybody who has bought into this way of thinking and living.

The Taken-for-Granted Ideas and Beliefs Informing Our Current Understanding of Leadership

In Western society there is a storehouse of ideas and beliefs about leaders that informs the expectations and fascination of followers/"ordinary" people (i.e., non-leaders) with the social construction called "leader". We take for granted that there is a distinction between leaders and followers/**ordinary people** (those perceived to have less or no power), and that there are certain expectations and roles that these two groups need to fulfil.

---

97 Walter Brueggemann's interview with Krista Tippett. See: http://being.publicradio.org/programs/2011/
prophetic-imagination/video-brueggemann_interview.shtml

This storehouse of ideas, beliefs and assumptions is supported by power. As asserted in an earlier chapter, power is neither good nor bad, nor is it located in a person. Power is negotiated between people in relationships and has real effects on people's lives. Leadership is thought of in a particular context of power, grounded in the ideas and beliefs that inform leaders.

PATRIARCHY

Patriarchy can be described as a 'social system in which men disproportionately occupy positions of power and authority, central norms and values are associated with manhood and masculinity (which in turn are defined in terms of dominance and control), and men are the primary focus of attention in most cultural spaces'.[98]

Patriarchy supports the notion of leadership in which the leader (male or female) is expected to provide, take care, make firm decisions and show the way forward, while having the best interests of the family/tribe in mind.[99] In this understanding of leadership the leader walks in front, faces the world out there, and cares and provides for the family or tribe. It means that the leader sometimes has to take tough decisions on behalf of a group – decisions the group may not necessarily agree with, but will later realise were good for them, like good medicine.

Some of the prevailing ideas on leadership within the understanding of patriarchy are that leaders

- have the final word or deciding vote
- have to make a decision in the end
- know better
- bring about the changes in life and in the world.

A very important notion within patriarchy is the idea that we need leaders to be the ones who have the final say about a matter – especially if we cannot agree on what is the right thing to do. When the decision is made, even if it was a joint decision by a community or company, this leader will be expected to take sole responsibility. S/he will be praised when the decision proves to be the right one, and blamed or even pushed out if the decision turns out to be wrong.

By virtue of their position and Western culture's fascination with this species, leaders have the power to speak about followers/ordinary people and decide for them. The construction of this kind of leader within patriarchy is a dance between the leader and the follower within the particular local culture and context. This understanding not only has implications for the leader, but constructs a particular kind of follower who is (and sometimes chooses to be) dependent

---

98 Johnson, A 2005. *The Gender Knot....*

99 In this description of patriarchy I refer to both men and women who practise leadership within the taken-for-granted beliefs and ideas of patriarchy.

on the leader's rule and providence for his/her wellbeing. This acceptance of the patriarchal understanding of leadership provides people with the space to abdicate all responsibility, accountability and commitment, since it fosters a sense of entitlement that has followers sitting around waiting for leaders, who they sometimes pay, to care for them in every way.

As a result, this kind of leadership positions and pushes leaders onto the world stage, while their followers (or anyone not in a leadership position) sit in the audience. Positioning leaders in this way thus renders them the only knowledgeable ones who can speak, decide and know for those in the audience. The implication is that the expectation for and creation of an alternative narrative and future rely on the leader, who should know all and be everything to everyone. Followers or ordinary people go one step further and not only expect care and a better future from their leaders, but also feel entitled to be provided for. Relying on one person alone leaves us with a thin description of a possible alternative future, one which is deprived of the richness of the gifts and histories of so-called ordinary people.

When a group/team/community has abdicated its participation in this world by handing over the rights to be participants in the creation of a new future to its leaders, those people frequently notice and pay attention to the presence/ absence of leaders in the conversation. The absence of leaders evokes responses in employees who emphasise that they have no influence or decision-making powers. If their leaders do not show them how to live the life or what to do, there is no point in them getting together or having a conversation. Management and leaders are seen as the ones who are paid to take responsibility, to be accountable and show commitment to change things for employees and citizens. Ordinary people or followers render themselves powerless and voiceless through their mere naming as "other", in regard to leaders. As a result, followers or ordinary people co-construct a limiting, abdicating and sometimes passive view of their participation in their dependency on leadership.

This limiting understanding of participation and abdication to leadership leaves no room for a counter-narrative which speaks of the rich knowledges, gifts and possibilities of communities, teams, organisations and institutions.

INDIVIDUALISM

Individualism is an ideology which emphasises "the moral worth of the individual" that promotes the exercise of one's goals and desires, and therefore values independence and self-reliance.[100] Within this understanding the individual becomes the ultimate point of reference and everything centres on the "I."

When the "I" is the central focus, leadership develops into the sole endeavour of the successful Lone Ranger who can single-handedly save and lead us all. Some of the prevailing ideas and beliefs which are informed by individualism, promote leaders as

---

100   See: http://en.wikipedia.org/wiki/Individualism

- somewhat above ordinary people in all aspects of their lives
- the ones who give up their humanity and show us all that they are better successful
- not allowed to speak in ways that reveal stories of vulnerability and struggle, unless they have overcome both
- possessing strengths and resources that set them above ordinary people.

According to Foucault, the "more one possesses power or privilege, the more one is marked as an individual".[101] Being marked as an individual elevates the leader above the rest of the community and gives them superhuman status. This leadership position comes with a tremendous ethical responsibility, as all decisions and speaking have powerful effects on people's lives.

The individualist mindset is always scanning the horizon for the Lone Ranger/ wonder-being who will single-handedly make everything better. Why else would we be so disappointed in leaders, unless we had super-human expectations of them? Followers idealise their leaders as long as they live up to their expectations; if they fail to do so, blame sets in.

Leaders are expected to live pure and exemplary lives, with perfect families and work-life balance. There is no recognition of their humanity (as part of the human community) unless they commit an immoral act (decided by society's values at the time) or are portrayed during an embarrassing moment. When this happens, people say that they are only human and the leaders may even say that about themselves. Followers expect individually marked super-human beings not to display any fallibility or fragility, and to be an example of success for us all.

David Epston explains that the requirements of a "ruthless individualism" are "determined by scores, marks, weights and other objective assessments of those norms which promise entry into the world of a 'successful person'".[102] Leaders are seen as the ultimate, successful people who have reached the top "I" position, and they are subjected to all forms of assessment and testing to ensure that they are the real deal.

Our fascination with the successful "I-leader" has rendered us blind to the collective, the communal and our connectedness with one another. In our blindness to the gift and possibility of our collective participation in the worlds we are co-constructing, we hop from leader to leader, allowing this leadership-dependency story to dominate our conversations and further reinforce our helplessness and lack of faith in anything ever changing in this world without them. Again we fall into waiting for leaders to create an alternative future, as we disregard the power of our communal relatedness, seeing and doing. In creating an alternative future there needs to be an emphasis on the successful "we" who collectively know more and can do more than the singular "I" can ever achieve.

---

101 Foucault, M 1977. *Discipline and Punish*, p. 192.

102 Epston, D. Up over, 177. See: http://www.narrativeapproaches.com/Book%20Folder/Down%20Under%20 Up%20Over/DE_UO_111-192.pdf

CONSUMERISM

Consumerism is a social and economic order based on fostering a desire to purchase goods and services in even greater quantities or amounts.[103] In an abstract sense, it is the belief that the free choice of consumers should dictate the economic structure of a society.

In Western society, where the "self" has become a commodity, buying goods in ever greater quantities so that the "self" will be developed and even more marketable and sellable has become the way to do business. The leader becomes a buyer of every possible product that will increasingly distinguish him/her from the rest. The leader buys knowledge and expertise from outside experts in order to get ahead.

Followers in this consumerist understanding outsource their rights and lives to leaders whom they pay to make things happen for them. Leaders are paid excessive amounts of money in the corporate field, and still significantly more than the rest of the workforce in government and NGOs. The monetary value assigned to leaders further heightens the expectations of those who pay them.

"The essential promise of consumerism," says community building author Peter Block, "is that all of what is fulfilling or needed in life can be purchased – from happiness to healing, from love to laughter, from raising a child to caring for someone at the end of life."[104] Not only have we bought into the idea of self as a commodity, we have bought into consumerism's promise that good leadership can be bought if we can only attend another workshop or sign up for yet another programme. As the newest leadership model promises to be the real thing, another round of leadership development takes its turn, leaving its mark of yet another unfulfilled promise. The promise of consumerism is a ruse, because not only can these important things not be bought, but the things we buy are temporal – they leave us with a sense that we have come one step closer, but yet again it is not enough, it is already outdated.

As followers within the consumerist society, we can easily discard leaders whom we dislike or disagree with, as we move our money to "buy" a leader we like more, or to whom we can outsource the task of making this world a better place. Yet again, the rich treasure chest of possibility of a community coming together without any price attached to it, is rendered obsolete as we outsource the possibility of an alternative future to the leaders we pay.

SO WHERE DOES THIS LEAVE US?

All these taken-for-granted ideas and beliefs inform our meaning making of the word and the world of leadership. The world and word construct stories about leaders and followers in a particular way that has real effects on what is possible

---

103   See: http://en.wikipedia.org/wiki/Consumerism

104   Block, P. See: http://www.yesmagazine.org/issues/what-happy-families-know/the-good-life-its-close-to-home

in our organisations and communities. These stories of leaders and followers are not only words on a page, but they have real consequences in our communities, societies, organisations and lives. Unpacking the assumptions and descriptions of the world which these leadership stories create, opens up the possibility to choose again. As we participate in this world, what are the constructions of leadership we want to be a part of?

What the Narrative Leadership Lens Is Not

Narrative leadership does not enter the debate and conversation about the flowers and leaves that have to grow from the tree of most of the bodies of knowledge on leadership. These conversations and ideas around leadership focus on the interior and exterior qualities of leadership, which are easily trapped in wrong/right and more successful/less successful characteristics and styles.

In terms of leadership, the Narrative lens does not

- provide a definition of leadership
- focus on a list of qualities and so-called inborn characteristics that determine the success of leaders
- enter into the debate about leaders being born or made
- expect leaders to be role models with the right answers
- expect leaders to have the skill to tell a good and compelling story to sell themselves or their cause
- come in a package with seven steps promising to turn leaders into the next Mandela or Gandhi
- buy into thin descriptions of a predictable world that produces leaders according to a recipe
- assume that the world in which we live creates sureness and certainty, which in turn produces leaders who recreate the expectation of such a world
- support the assumption that a one-size-fits-all leader will bring true leadership for every generation, for all time, in all contexts and cultures.

Narrative Leadership as an Alternative

Narrative leadership offers a counter-narrative that reconstructs the current notions of leadership. It is not a new model, with new, distinct characteristics and qualities. It proposes a lens, a way of being, seeing, engaging and participating in this world, that invites a different relationship for the leader within a context and with a so-called follower. As we create worlds through language, as a society we have constructed the words "leader" and "leadership" to mean specific things in a particular time and culture. Our current understanding of leadership is a construction that has gone beyond what is possible. Perhaps we should be imagining a different word to celebrate our reconstruction of the notion of leadership, but until we collectively find a new term that better describes our reconstruction, the meaning and understanding brought with the name "Narrative leadership" will have to do.

Narrative leadership is the description of a lens that informs practices and skills born from the alternative ground and foundational assumptions about human beings, narratives, language, relationships, societal beliefs and ideas, power, authorship, community and possibility. Growing from these foundational assumptions, Narrative leadership is the craft of bringing people together in transformational conversations where their human uniqueness, imagination, giftedness, and knowledges and skills of living are welcomed and invited to participate.

The Narrative lens provides a way to see and engage with the meaning leaders have made about this word and the world, and how that impacts their life narratives. It opens up choice for the kind of leadership story that leaders prefer, and enables them to define the task of leadership for themselves, which in turn opens up a multiplicity of leadership stories.

This particular lens on leadership understands and supports the craft and art of building relationships with the community, team or organisation, through transformational listening, asking questions and providing a welcoming space.

LEADING WITH HUMAN BEINGS SEEN AS GIFTED

Human beings lead extraordinary and exotic lives. This means they are unique and have an abundance of narratives, histories and gifts that open up the imagination of who they are and what they can become.

If the team/community/organisation comprises extraordinary and gifted human beings, it sets leaders free from the pressure of having something (usually called development) in mind for those they lead. The Narrative lens relieves leaders of a kind of seeing, a gaze, in which they magically know what is good and right for their followers. This kind of seeing and knowing sets them apart from the rest of humanity in terms of their accomplishment. The Narrative lens is an invitation for leaders to rejoin the ranks of humanity, since we collectively lead extraordinary lives.

INVITATIONS TO ACCOUNTABILITY AND COMMITMENT

The Narrative lens enables leaders to come alongside teams/boards/communities and organisations, by listening and asking questions about what the persons/communities have in mind for themselves. Knowledge and what can be known are not the sole responsibility of the leader, because so-called ordinary people bring their own knowledges and giftedness to an organisation, and this collaborative knowing becomes a collective act. The invitation to participate in the co-creation of knowledge invites in practices of responsibility and accountability as we co-construct knowledge together.

Leading then becomes something leaders do *with* groups/teams/communities and not a responsibility that is taken up on behalf of, *for* and *over* others.

USING THE POWER AND PRIVILEGE WITHIN A LEADERSHIP POSITION

Within the Narrative seeing, leaders are invited to an awareness of the power that their position brings and intentionally deconstruct their power and decentre themselves within this position. This means that leaders are conscious of their own humanity and invite this quality into the room with people they work or journey with.

If leaders use their power in this way it will not necessarily make them popular, as some people still prefer the superhuman façade that comes with the position in Western society. As a result, the Narrative lens is inherently counter-cultural, because it allows those in leadership positions to see beyond society's deep longing for the Lone Ranger leader of the masses, who takes full responsibility for fixing and saving us all.

In addition, the Narrative leadership work enables individuals to use their power to create spaces and places for the narratives and voices of those society might call ordinary, powerless or voiceless to enter. Within this approach, leaders invite ordinary/powerless/voiceless people/employees into a conversation where their participation is valued, and their wisdom and expertise are handled with equal care. The task of the leader within this approach is to ensure that everybody feels welcome, connected, listened to and is invited to participate.

The task of the leader within the Narrative understanding is to

- stand with people in the possibilities that would create an alternative future
- use the power and privilege that come with the position in our societies to create alternative ways of speaking and asking questions
- challenge and question the practices and ideas which we have taken for granted that are no longer useful or helpful and are even harmful. An example is to challenge those practices and ideas that dehumanise people and make them into slaves and docile bodies
- invite participants to take back the storytelling rights of their narratives that would result in their authorship moving into the transformation of all they engage with
- come alongside people by amplifying and giving voice to the alternative and counter-narrative that is always on the way and rising up
- create a space for people to explore empowerment possibilities that they are interested in and that are not prescribed by the leader as the developmental path
- use their power and privilege to come alongside each individual's unique sense of agency and act as a community for them.

AN AWARENESS OF ONE'S OWN LEADERSHIP STORIES

The lens of Narrative leadership enables leaders to be aware of the important life stories that inform them, and by which they prefer to live and see the world and their work. In this description of leadership there is no right or wrong story a leader should tell or live from. These leadership stories are informed by each leader's own values, gifts, knowledges and skills.

In this construction of leadership, leading with your own story is an acknowledgement of your own humanity that allows and invites the extraordinary humanity of others to enter.

LEADERSHIP SEEING PROBLEMS ANEW

The Narrative lens provides leaders with the skill to see the problem as the problem. This understanding invites a community, team or organisation to stand collectively against problems in collaboration with one another, and is not based on finding the one and only culprit to shame and blame.

The dominant story of the blame culture in organisations is so prevalent because in our society we often move on when we can answer the question "Who's to blame?" The answer to this question then absolves us from participating in the problem story and hands it down to the guilty one (meaning the one who was supposed to be in charge). As we blame leaders we can rest and move on with our lives, as we never have to answer the question about society's and our own participation in the problem stories. This way of thinking is entrenched in individualist ideas because it fosters the notion that life would be much better if we could only identify the guilty one. As a result we never ask the question how we colluded in constructing the problem, how we are influencing the problem and, in some cases, how we are benefiting from the problem story.

This approach to leadership walks away from blame and walks towards a communal understanding of problems and the re-writing thereof. Leaders within this approach understand and speak about problems in a different way, that positions problems as a problem story with which we stand in a relationship and which we can collectively re-write if we choose to do so. This practice has no need to solve the problem but invites a new relationship with the problem and as a result lives into the possibility of an alternative counter-narrative.

LEADERSHIP CREATING NEW WORLDS THROUGH LANGUAGE

The Narrative work, with its emphasis on how we speak and language our world, opens up the possibility of seeing what our speaking is creating, where it is informed from, who benefits and what it then produces. When the nature of our speaking and listening is co-opted in the language of patriarchy and individualism, it will be recreating the very world we are challenging.

Leaders are able to change the world with communities as we collectively shift and change the language through our way of speaking. As we become intentional about the language we use to describe and participate in the world, we are no longer only describing the world, but re-authoring and re-writing it through our way of speaking and, in so doing, are developing an alternative language.

The word "leader" is created in language, and within the uniqueness and giftedness of each leader this word can be recreated and more richly described with values and qualities that live into the possibility of each leader. If leaders are in a space to validate their own experience in the language they have "created", it is indeed possible to speak in new ways as they create new possibilities in language. Imagine how powerful it would be if leaders provided a space to co-create a new language and way of speaking in their communities and organisations.

The Narrative lens offers a means for leaders to see and understand that our worlds are created through language and can be recreated through language. When leaders are aware of this and able to see that the world around them has been negotiated and created in language, they become participants with communities, teams and organisations in re-writing and re-authoring their world. Leaders with this understanding are aware of how and what they speak, they know that they are creating the world they are living in.

LEADERS AS INTERPRETIVE BEINGS

Within the Narrative approach, leaders are aware of the lens though which they view their leadership and what that means for their life and their work in the world. They are clear about the meaning they have made of the word and the world that opens when they talk about leadership. They are interested in the meaning making of those they engage and work with.

NARRATIVES ON THE MOVE

Narrative leadership work is aware that the narrative can change at any given moment and is open to explorations and questions to more richly describe this movement. This skill enables leaders to know and understand that the world is not as certain and predictable as they were told.

LEADERS CONSTRUCTED WITHIN RELATIONSHIP

This approach to leadership is a dance of collaboration that knows that the idea of leadership is constructed in relationship with those who are being led. Together, we construct what this means for us. There is a dance between the leader and the follower that co-constructs what it means to be both. Participants in this construction are the taken-for-granted beliefs and ideas in a particular society about what leadership is (this can be helpful, or not). In the end, the leader and the follower make up this relationship as they go along, and therefore conversations are crucial for clarifying the meaning, challenges and possibilities of the relationship.

LEADING WITH

Leadership is not seen as an individual endeavour where the focus is on the leader alone getting it right. Within this understanding, leadership is seen as a co-

construction through relationships, where the leader is constructed in the loving support of a community that leads with him/her. Therefore, teams, communities and organisations are not seen as objects that have to buy into the leader's vision, but are seen as gifted, knowledgeable and able to contribute, co-construct and co-create a vision and alternative world together with the leader.

In this alternative story of leadership the so-called ordinary people are invited into the conversation as knowledgeable and as able to equally contribute. As a result, the distinctions between leaders and ordinary people fade and blur into emergence. In this collaboration the so-called leader becomes part of the conversation, in whatever form. When we refuse to live into the distinctions between leaders and ordinary people, it is no longer a question of whether we should include them (ordinary people); it becomes the way we dare to convene, listen, know and do, together, in our communal relatedness.

NARRATIVE LEADERSHIP IN ACTION: *THE JOURNEY INTO THE MYSTERY OF GREAT LOVE*

Here is an example of an alternative approach to leadership in action, displayed as a team of leaders dares to convene, listen, know and do together from a deep sense of communal relatedness.

As I was thinking and writing about the Narrative work as a lens on leadership, I was invited into an amazing community of Catholic sisters from the Congregation of St. Joseph. In 2007, seven separate congregations of St. Joseph, all situated in the American Midwest, with seven distinct characters and stories, came together to create one new congregation.

The mission of this congregation is to live and work so that all people may be united with God and with one another. In unifying love, they serve the dear neighbour to whom they are committed through their charism (the gift of the Spirit) and Generous Promises.[105]

The Congregation of St. Joseph decided to choose seven leaders, called the Congregation Leadership Team (CLT), to embark on a journey that would co-lead the congregation. The choice of shared leadership clearly questions the assumption that hierarchical leadership is the only way. Therefore, it puts them at odds with the hierarchical structures in the church. These leaders, together with members of their congregation, dared to imagine an alternative narrative, a counter-narrative to leadership that has set them on the stage of the religious world from which they serve.

As part of a Vatican-mandated Apostolic Visitation of all 400 congregations of US Catholic Sisters, five delegates came "on site for a visit" in December of 2010. The stated purpose of this visit was a concern about "the quality of life" of the sisters. The delegates' agenda was to inquire about congregational practices and beliefs. Clear that they had nothing to hide and eager to tell the story of the new

---

105 See: http://www.csjoseph.org/our_mission_vision.aspx

congregation, 139 of the 700 sisters volunteered to be interviewed by one of the five delegates. The visitors were overwhelmed by the number of volunteers!

Prior to this on-site visit, the CLT was expected to complete a questionnaire from the Apostolic Visitation Office (as were the leaders of the 400+ other congregations of Sisters in the US). After carefully discerning its content, the CLT came to believe the questionnaire did not allow them to share the real story of how their sisters live and serve in 21st-century America. The CLT declined to complete the questionnaire and responded instead by sending to the Apostolic Visitation Office documents they believed more adequately described the life, spirituality and mission of the Congregation of St. Joseph.

During the time when the Vatican was investigating individual congregations of US Sisters, it also conducted a "doctrinal assessment" of the Leadership Conference of Women Religious (LCWR), an organisation to which the Congregation of St. Joseph and the CLT belong. The LCWR consists of more than 1 500 members who lead more than 80 per cent of the 57 000 women religious in the US. The seven leaders of the Congregation of St. Joseph belong to the LCWR.

When I visited the CLT in April 2012, they had just received the results of the doctrinal assessment of the LCWR and learned that the Vatican had mandated a five-year reform of the LCWR. With the leaders of other US congregations of Catholic Sisters who belong to the LCWR, the CLT is involved in a discernment process designed to determine how the LCWR will respond to this mandate.

This is the context in which these seven women are practising a kind of leadership which this chapter describes, and which I only imagined and dreamt was possible. They are seven extraordinary leaders, not because they have innate characteristics, strengths and resources that set them apart from the rest of the congregation. They have been leading in an extraordinary way with the congregation, as, collectively, this spiritual community has dared to shift the story of leadership and followers. They live into a leading, discerning and loving together that brings with it a shift of what is possible for congregations as religious communities.

I was privileged to spend an afternoon with the CLT and asked them about their leadership journey. Their description was further supported by a visit to one of the congregation's centres in Chicago, where I experienced 80+ of their sisters gathered for an annual assembly. We are only at the beginning of our journey of richly describing their approach to leadership, but the following account gives a taste of the possibilities and alternative ways of being that this approach to leadership opens up and is built upon. After describing the leadership team's responses to my questions, we reflect on the possibilities of this alternative leadership narrative.

NAMING THE LEADERSHIP JOURNEY

What would you name this journey of leadership that you have been creating and participating in?

When I asked the leadership team to name the journey that they are on, several offerings were given, like New Life, God's Great Gift/Love, Mystery of Grace, Uncharted Journey, New Horizons and Drawn by a Dream. The team decided on *The Journey into the Mystery of Great Love* as a title that captures the experience for the moment. After giving the leadership journey its name, we spoke about the story of leadership with this title for the rest of our time together.

THE INFLUENCE OF THE LEADERSHIP JOURNEY

How has The Journey into the Mystery of Great Love influenced you as leaders?

- It has taken us to a new realm of risk taking
- It has given us love, life and energy
- It has helped us to make hard decisions differently, as we paid attention to what we would surrender and let go of
- It has invited edge-members to join us on the way
- We have been able to repurpose everything we do
- We have been paying even more attention to our relationships
- We have faith in one another in the journey we are on
- We are clear that we can give no guarantees
- The influence on us and from us has extended far beyond our membership.

Each of these reflections of the influence of this leadership journey could be further explored with stories and moments in the history of this team – evidence and explorations of the possibilities of co-leading with a congregation.

THE TAKEN-FOR-GRANTED IDEAS AND BELIEFS THAT ARE CHALLENGED

This alternative *Journey into the Mystery of Great Love* lives in a world that thinks in a different way about leadership and followers, with totally different expectations.

The Roman Catholic Church is one of the oldest patriarchal institutions in the world. It is a religious institution where women have not been granted a voice equal to that of males. In this patriarchal understanding of leadership, members look to the top to act and the bishops are its spokespersons. Power is centralised in Rome.

Below are the taken-for-granted ideas and beliefs that these leaders could think of in their exploration of the following question:

What are the taken-for-granted ideas and beliefs within your religious context around leadership that The Journey into the Mystery of Great Love is challenging?

- Live life separately from the world
- Leadership is hierarchical

- The direction in which we are heading is fixed and clear
- There is a divide between the sacred and the secular
- Leaders have the answers
- The world out there is dangerous
- Business, pragmatic and economic efficiency come first
- Leaders enforce decisions
- Wisdom lies in a few
- There is one right way
- Everyone is in one place called the corporate office.

Most of these ideas and beliefs have survived over centuries, and the sisters of the Congregation of St. Joseph are daring to live a counter-narrative that challenges all the notions of leadership and hierarchy that have been a given for so long.

Whom Do We Authorise to Speak?

Taken-for-granted ideas and beliefs are supported by people and institutions with power and authority, who are the advocates and voice of most ideas on leadership. The advocates of these ideas work, act and live from these understandings and expect others to live accordingly, as explored in the preceding section.

The leadership team mentioned the business world, the Institutional Church, its tradition and early formation in the life of nuns as advocates for these ways of being a leader in their religious context.

The Beliefs and Ideas Informing the Alternative Narrative

What informs The Journey into the Mystery of Great Love and gives it life?

With this question we explored the alternative ideas and beliefs that inform their story of leadership:

- Shared leadership
- We are one
- To open our lives
- We are in it together
- Freedom to live with ambiguity and organically
- Relationships as primary
- Multiple values
- Making mistakes
- Wisdom lies in the body
- Trying things and experimenting as we learn from these without blaming
- Embracing new information

- Sharing responsibility with lay colleagues
- A readiness to create with discernment
- Co-creating a new culture
- Inviting people in

Again, all of the ideas and beliefs mentioned above can be further explored in terms of events, knowledges, relationships and stories that have made this possible.

In a conversation with congregational members at La Grange (in Chicago), the following reflections emerged to further support the ideas and beliefs of the leadership team:

- We are communing neighbour with neighbour, and neighbour with God, regardless of whether this person is a member of the Catholic Church
- There is a mutuality in which we experience God
- Unifying love is something we seek out, create and minister from
- The charism helps us see where the unifying love is happening and helps us to present it in such a way that unity is the outflow that is constructed
- Our mission is to create harmony and unity where there is none
- Whenever there is disunity we work towards creating unity
- Our prophetic calling is to meet the needs of the world
- We serve to love
- We are called to love God and love our neighbour, without distinction
- We align ourselves with those who are oppressed
- The favourite name for God is love, not God as Father, Son or Holy Spirit. It is an inclusive love that pours itself out and unites all of creation
- These ideas are built on the bigger "us" that is inclusive of everybody, even those outside of the Catholic Church.

The ideas of both the leadership and the congregational members co-create a different world of leadership, followers, community, service and the other.

WHO IS AUTHORISED TO SPEAK ABOUT THE ALTERNATIVE NARRATIVE OF LEADERSHIP?

The leadership team reflected on the members of their community of concern whom they have authorised to speak about who they are as a leadership team. Primarily, this leadership team authorises their sisters to speak. They have given some people the authorisation to write about their style of leadership, but have not authorised them to speak in their name or on their behalf. The list includes: Vatican II education, the feminist movement, women in leadership, Peter Block, Margaret Wheatley, Chené Swart, whoever works with them, everyone who is a spiritual seeker, and all of them as leaders. Since its mandated reform was announced, the LCWR has received thousands of letters of support from people all around the world, from Catholics and from people of many other faith traditions. Some priests and bishops have also expressed their support for and encouragement to the LCWR.

During this same time frame, the Congregation of St. Joseph also received letters and emails expressing the support of people who took the opportunity to share their story of how they benefited from their ministries. These groups of people form a community of concern around US Catholic Sisters in general. Their support, care and curiosity further thicken the alternative story of *The Journey into the Mystery of Great Love* of the Congregation of St. Joseph.

What Is This Alternative Story Saying?

Given that my time with this leadership team came just after they heard the news regarding the mandated reform of the LCWR, I asked:

What is The Journey into the Mystery of Great Love saying to the Vatican?

- Look at us
- Talk with us
- Don't be afraid that we want to be in an equal relationship
- It is the same Gospel that we are trying to live
- It is the same Jesus we love
- We cannot go backwards
- I am a new person
- We respond to the needs of the people
- It is about the Gospel
- We must be about our Father's business
- We love this church and are being faithful to it.

These sentences and phrases are all invitations into a richer description of how this approach to leadership reacts and speaks to those who think differently about leadership.

I had a wonderful conversation with Kathy Sherman, a musician who composes songs for the congregation.[106] I asked her whether a song had come to her during these times. She sang me a beautiful song called "Love Cannot Be Silenced".

An Alternative Narrative on Leadership

In the Congregation of St. Joseph's approach to leadership, seven leaders co-lead with the congregation. This approach does not have control in mind and is grounded in an untraditional set of ideas and beliefs. The leaders are co-creating and making up congregational life with the sisters of the congregation. They are bringing their visions of leadership, and together they are co-constructing a vision of leadership.

---

106 See: http://www.youtube.com/watch?v=_OzLhTV6pkQ

These leaders do not enter with answers, as they do not claim to know everything and about everything equally, although there are still some expectations on the part of congregational members for them to act as the experts. This leadership team redirects issues and challenges to the right person or group. When somebody asks them something, especially when it is done in the old paradigm of "you are the leader", they think with this person about who would be the right person to talk to. They also give options that congregational members can work through before making a decision. They always invite congregational members to take ownership of the congregation, as everybody is collectively responsible for the congregation.

Because this approach to leadership is not about control or about being right, the team easily apologises for and is sorry about things they might not have handled in a way that was helpful. Given other approaches to leadership, this mode is fragile, as it is on the way of making sense and meaning with those whom they are leading.

The leadership team is a circle of leaders who think with one another and with the congregation about current affairs and about the future. They share the responsibility of leading the congregation, and therefore often decide in discernment with the congregation on important matters. Such discerning together informs how the congregation should be and what they should do. They believe that they can come to a decision with the congregation and have authorised everybody in the congregation to speak freely and to participate, as inclusivity and mutuality are strong values.

This community of leaders is intentional about moving around to build relationships with the congregation, and therefore its work includes a great deal of travel. "It's all about relationships," the leaders say.

In the end, this leadership team knows that they have co-constructed and are co-constructing change and transformation of which they will most probably not see the final outcome.

The Congregation of St. Joseph's leadership story gives us hope for an alternative way of being leaders and followers, through whom collective responsibility and accountability can flow over into re-authoring the worlds and communities we live in and are called to serve in. However, the Narrative lens on leadership does not promise to be an approach that will be useful to all people in all situations at all times. It does not claim to be better than contemporary and familiar approaches.

Narrative work as a lens on leadership does offer leaders an opportunity to engage in transformational listening, questioning and convening to

- understand and make sense of their own narrative from which they lead
- convene teams, communities, companies and groups in ways that can shift the conversation
- name a problem story and facilitate the transformation of stories into new and preferred counterstories
- celebrate their own humanity, gifts, competencies and skills, and those of the people they lead
- construct appropriate rituals of celebrations and communities that celebrate
- have an altered ethic of seeing human beings
- challenge current dominant notions and constructions of leadership that are no longer useful or helpful
- understand that they construct their worlds through language and as they name their story, they can choose again
- understand and challenge the societal taken-for-granted-ideas and beliefs that enable leaders to see what they can see
- gather and convene people in a way that deconstructs and decentres their power and privilege
- engage with language as a way to construct what is possible in the conversation
- co-create transformation in the way they listen and ask questions
- engage people in intimate ways through the invitation of their narratives in the room
- co-construct and co-create an alternative and counter-narrative that opens up the possibility for people to choose their freedom and live into an alternative future.

In this Narrative approach to leadership, every conversation and every meeting is part of a counter-narrative, as we re-author the world through our language, our relationships, the use of power, the challenging of confining and harmful ideas, and our choice for constructing an alternative narrative that ripples into transforming the world as we know it.

CHAPTER TWELVE

NARRATIVE CONSULTING

Narrative consulting practices come alongside work-communities to harvest and explore the rich multiplicity of stories, gifts, values, hopes and dreams, with respect and curiosity. The process embraces a way of "being with", whereby the Narrative consultant comes alongside in the re-writing of alternative preferred stories in organisations.

A Narrative consultant is an expert at facilitating a particular kind of respectful discussion and conversation. In this conversation the voice, knowledges, gifts and narratives of the client are invited and play a central role in what is discussed and how it is discussed.

Counter to the Narrative consulting approach, the predominant understanding of the word "consultant" in our society is of a person who provides outside professional or expert advice, analysis and solutions. Within this understanding, the consultant knows and tells the client what is wrong, what needs to be fixed, and what will happen if it is not fixed in the prescribed manner. The consultant as expert does things *for* the organisation as the one who knows best. The task of a consultant in this understanding is to speak for, to, about and on behalf of an organisation, and to present a complete list of recommendations for the way forward. This expert approach to consulting reduces the participation of the community of workers to mere informants of the evidence of problems which consultants are interested in fixing or advising on. The gaze of the expert scans the landscapes and horizons of the organisation and then speaks from these knowledges and insights. This approach can, however, hinder the implementation of expert consultant-driven initiatives and can cause stagnation in the organisational culture, due to the lack of buy-in and participation by those who have not been included in the consultation.

In the Narrative approach the client or organisation is viewed as a community of workers or work-communities, not as a workforce. The **work-community** speaks about and to the idea that not only do people come to work, produce, serve and ensure profit, but they are also a community of human beings, working together to earn a living and co-create a working environment that is in line with their values, hopes and dreams for the future. On all levels, the community of workers is seen as key informants and contributors to what is known and can be known in the future (i.e., the vision) of the organisation.

Narrative consultants are aware of, take notice of and engage with the taken-for-granted beliefs and ideas that inform what is possible or not possible within an organisation. These taken-for-granted beliefs and ideas often render the unique gifts, histories and values of the work-communities as unimportant, or as the exception to the rule. In addition to facilitating and inviting the knowledges and expertise of the community of workers to enter, a Narrative consultant is a "**documentalist**" of these narratives, histories, gifts and knowledges.[107] These documents richly describe a counter-story which serves as a springboard for the dreams and hopes that the community of workers has in mind for the organisation. This story of possibility stands as an alternative to the dominant stories of deficiencies, analyses and solutions often told within organisations and by external consultants.

Consulting With the Narrative Approach in South Africa

Any consultant enters an organisation with tremendous power, given the dominant expert belief and expectation created within the consulting industry. Narrative consultants enter with an awareness of this power, influenced by the organisation's expectations. Approaching with the Narrative lens and practices influences how, with what and where we enter an organisation, which allows us to see so much more than problems that need to be fixed. In addition, we enter organisations knowing that the specific and local context is constructed by the particularities of the history of that organisation, within the larger story of the taken-for-granted ideas and beliefs of the national history and culture.

In journeying with companies in South Africa I have found that the Narrative approach has many connections with the gifts and challenges of our 11 official languages, as well with the alternative narrative we are constructing. The stories here illustrate the use of Narrative consulting practices in that context.

The Story of Difference

In South Africa at present diversity is a given, but for most of us who grew up in the time when apartheid was the dominant story, the life we knew was identified by sameness. We were warned against anybody who was different from us in any way. "Keep to your own," we were told right from an early age. Now we are confronted, especially in our cities and in the workplace, with the other.

The history of our differences and the institutionalisation of those differences through apartheid have left us with the problem story that most of the country's citizens have never had an opportunity to sit in the same room and have conversations with the other/a stranger in terms of race, gender, educational levels, class, language, age, etc. As a nation we have multiple taken-for-granted ideas about other ethnic groups, and about people from different levels of work in organisations. These notions, coupled with our history, invite a story of stuckness and trappedness in conversations that do not take us forward.

---

107 "Documentalist" is another word I learned from Pierre Blanc-Sahnoun during one of our conversations about the Narrative practices in working with organisations.

In workshops, the story of difference and divide between white and black South Africans often plays out in the seating in the room. A few open chairs in-between black and white participants leave no doubt that we are segregated and different from one another, and from different worlds. In our country the story of our segregating differences has been constructed over so many years that we seldom pause to question the numerous times when it was not true. Even more subtle is the story of divide among South Africans from different ethnic groups, and the huge divide between black South Africans and people from the rest of Africa. A very elusive dividing story shows up in the differences between English- and Afrikaans-speaking white South Africans, grounded in the history of the Anglo-Boer War.

We are steeped in the history and stories of our cultures and in South Africa, the story of apartheid weaves through our sense making as it has institutionalised the story of difference in a violent manner. When we reflect in workshops on what we have lost through the institutionalised discrimination of apartheid, participants voice that we lost relationships, conversation and communication with the other. But, despite the well-documented story of apartheid creating loss of identity and community, counter-stories of the Rainbow Nation are the seedbed for the possibilities we are now living into as a nation. One example of such a counter-story tells of a white mine manager who dared to, on occasion, invite a black miner (in a time when he could have paid a severe price for doing this) into his home for whiskey, to share their dreams for the future.

The institutionalised story of difference in South Africa also beckoned us into a language and naming of the other. In honest conversations our histories, stereotypes, language and assumptions about the other enter, and with them a whole world of meaning. This naming of our differences has sent us off into different orbits, never to consider that we have anything in common – not even our basic human experience. We can, therefore, dismiss the other in the blink of an eye. This dismissing is based on our histories and truth claims about the world and the different cultures as we know and see them.

Narrative practices provide a way for South Africans to see one another anew and afresh. This approach provides us with an understanding of how we make meaning through the language of the other. It gives us eyes to see and a way to speak about the taken-for-granted beliefs and ideas that inform this othering. We can comprehend how these ideas and beliefs have distanced us from one another, as we so easily identify our fellow human beings as the other based on language, gender, race, age and class. The Narrative lens enables us to collectively see what we have constructed about one another and is a political stance, meaning that the manner in which we have the conversation and what we talk about, show that we are already living the counter-narrative and challenging the problem story. The Narrative work then offers us an invitation to choose again whether or not we want to continue living into the separating, labelling and judging stories we have about one another.

THE POST-COLONIAL STORY

Our post-colonial history brought with it ideas and beliefs of white supremacy and an emphasis that knowledge and expertise lie with the white European. As we still live with the residue of these regimes and their ideas, the Narrative consulting work offers practices that do not re-institutionalise and perpetuate the very thing we want to challenge and live away from.

I attended a workshop in South Africa where a white consultant chose an African song to be sung by all participants, without knowing the meaning or the history of the song. After the song had been sung by most of those present, the room fell silent. Then a black woman stood up and explained that she had not joined in the singing because the song was usually sung at the funerals of comrades who died during the apartheid struggle. She believed there were other songs we could sing together, that could take our country into a new story. This is a classic example of white people's notions of superiority. We still think, at times, that we are doing good as we continue to know *for* others and do not search to know *with* them.

We invite these colonial ideas back when we, as consultants and facilitators, create spaces where we come in as the experts and presume and present ourselves as the ones who know about individuals and communities more than they know about themselves. We silence them when we correct their words and language with patronising sentences such as: "So what you are really saying is...." Often we then complete the sentence with our own words and language that are filled with power and loaded with meaning which is foreign to other work-communities. The recipient/client nods to signify that, surely, what the consultant just said sounds much more impressive, because communities do not always know or feel free to express what they think about what just happened, or what someone's observation really means.

The Narrative practices see the client/community/organisation as the expert and respect their knowledges, traditions, language, histories and gifts. Practitioners enter with a not-knowing approach, where the meaning of even the most obvious act, word or behaviour is not assumed.

THE STORY OF RECONCILIATION

In South Africa we have the unique challenge that, as people of difference, we have never had the opportunity to "see" one another. We still live with many labels and great aversion towards the other, meaning anyone who is different from us. The Narrative work helps us to access the grace to listen to the stories of the other, and invites our own narratives to be transformed in the listening, as we live without judgement or condemnation of the other.

I have seen numerous narratives shifting into stories of reconciliation as our common humanity is embraced, the commonalities of our stories are marvelled at, assumptions and ideas and beliefs are exposed, and then great joy and wonder have emerged. The Narrative work offers a transformational process of reconciliation and a place to celebrate the possibility of collectively discovering the mystery and hope of the alternative narrative.

One example of a story of reconciliation, seeing and transformation, happened in a workshop with a team from the protection services department at a platinum mine. The team consisted of a few white male Afrikaner employees who had served as policemen during the apartheid period, a few old illiterate black men who had been employed on the mines for over 20 years, as well as younger black men and women. At the end of one of our sessions a middle-aged black man said he was going to let racism go, and that he was willing to live into a new narrative about what this team could become. Two weeks later I saw the team again and asked them what gifts they had received from one another in the interim. The black man who had spoken at the end of the last session raised his hand first, and pointed at a white manager, saying that when this manager shared the story of his sick father with him he felt like a real human being for the first time in his life. After hearing this story, the team shared unique outcomes in the form of gifts for nearly an hour, and named their new narrative *We are Family*!

These were my reflections on the experience of this day:

The day the Sun came
We were sitting innocently in a circle when the light of gifts entered
First slowly, but very direct
Looking one another in the eye as human becomings
"I want to give....a gift

You have told me about your father's sickness and I felt like a real human being
You listened to me
You are a father to me
You have really helped me
You have changed so much
You have given me friendliness"
And on and on it went

Wave upon wave of belonging and connectedness flowing through all of us
Tears of gratefulness to be a witness of and to the transformations
Of the body
The soul
The mind
The community

And then the Father/Uncle (no longer the manager) of the team that is now a community

Gave a gift to us, the witnesses and co-creators of the space:

"You have not turned this into a political space where we fight about the past and who is/was right

*You have helped us to see one another as human beings
And this is the gift you are to us"*

*As I was still wiping away the tears, the group calls eagerly for us to come outside
and see the Parhelion*

*A luminous rainbow halo surrounding the sun in midday South Africa, right above
our meeting place*

*And so the ice crystals came to dance above our heads in utter summer heat being
the alternative story in a harsh reality called Base Metal*

*The platinum dust of our joy and connectedness merging into the white of the
parhelic circle*

THE STORY OF COMMUNITY

Black African cultures have a very strong focus on community, and in the storytelling this focus continuously shows up. The Narrative approach is grounded in communal understanding that respects the rich histories of a community, which inform our narratives. Numerous participants have remarked that after a Narrative process where respect for story and community are celebrated, it feels like home and family.

In a teambuilding conversation a Nigerian man engaged in rich gift-giving to his group members as he told each a story around the gift he had received from them. He came to me afterwards and his eyes were smiling when he said he could now come to work as a member of the team because these conversations and connections felt like a "child was born today!" This demonstrates the way Narrative work enables people from communal cultures to reconnect with their communal background, as the telling and re-telling of narratives help them to feel and be connected to the teams they engage with.

When my African brothers and sisters tell their stories, there is always a moment when their eyes light up in remembering a community of people who supported them in their journey. Their reflections tell of how they are now giving back to these communities in gratitude for what was given to them. This strong sense of communal living is a dominant theme in most black communities, where sharing and caring for extended family are not just normal, but a given.

Within our economic system after apartheid, a number of black African families have now been included in the growing middle class. This has taken some of them out of their communities, and others who chose to stay in their communities have been moving to wealthier parts of their townships. The conversations around the other are thus also conversations around classism and how we sometimes think we are better than others based on our education, opportunities and the things we have. A young man once told me how, after being part of a workshop where he came to understand some of these harmful taken-for-granted ideas and beliefs, he no longer practised classism in his community. He again shows up in his community by engaging and helping whenever he sees a tent being pitched for a funeral.

In our Western world with its strong notions around individualism, the Narrative work offers a way of seeing organisations, teams and groups as communities; we then refer to them as a work-community, a community of students or managers, and so forth. The moment the word "community" is introduced, it invites notions of care, collective wisdom and knowledges, gifts and neighbourliness to enter a world that is so often rooted in assumptions of competition, success, hoarding knowledge, and doing it my way as the only way.

I was invited to conduct a workshop for final-year students at a local university, with the goal that they needed to now know how to start acting "professionally", since they would be entering the workplace within the next year. As the group engaged in conversations with one another I constantly referred to them as a community of students. In the final reflections, one of the students remarked that when she started the course she used to access completed papers from previous exams that she hid away, not wanting to share them with the other students. Her eyes opened in the workshop to see the participants as a community of students who can assist one another, learn from one another and collectively do well as a class.

The Narrative work takes hands with the notion of community in all its forms. It reconnects with its importance and celebrates communities that stand with people as they embark on the alternative and counter-story of their lives.

THE STORY OF ORGANISATIONAL LIFE

Peter Block speaks about various taken-for-granted beliefs and ideas that play into the discussion between a consultant and an organisation that are important to grasp, be aware of and challenge.[108] He explains that organisations inevitably dehumanise people because they value people less and less. Peter explains that what dehumanises organisations are the system's design and requirements based on predictability, consistency, control and outcomes.

The idea that organisations are dehumanising shows up in their systems, which equate human beings with machines and expect them to produce and ensure profit as they give everything to the organisation. There is no place for human fallibility and fragility within these systems. This deep longing for consistency and predictability wipes anything that is unique out of its way.

The Narrative work stands against and in the presence of these harmful taken-for-granted ideas and beliefs that want to dehumanise work-communities into machine-like entities that embody perfection and predictability. The gifts the

---

108 Restoring humanity in our communities and institutions. An interview with Peter Block. See: http://www.peterblock.com/_assets/downloads/Converse8%20Peter%20Block.pdf

Narrative consultant brings are the questions and the curiosity that will expose the harmful and limiting ideas and assumptions operating within an organisation. In addition, the effects of these ideas and assumptions are also examined, exposed and reflected upon, which leads to conversations of responsibility and accountability for what the work-community now knows about these ideas and beliefs. The Narrative consultant could ask questions such as:

- "What ideas and assumptions constitute organisational life?
- Whose ideas are they?
- How, why and by whom were such ideas produced?
- Who benefits from their circulation and whose voices are marginalised?"[109]

In addition to exposing the taken-for-granted ideas and beliefs as well as the language that informs an organisation, the Narrative work also focuses on the alternative stories that are lived in spite of them.

When a Narrative consultant enquires about the uniqueness of the story, and the gifts and competencies of an organisation, and does not speak the language of certainty and predictability, the process stands against the known and given world of ideas that inform organisations. This work expectantly scans the horizons for those moments in time when unique, sparkling events told of extraordinary gifts, resilience, knowledges and faith of the community of workers. As long as human beings work within organisations, I believe, like Foucault, that political resistance is not just possible but a necessary part of the equation, and that "one must put 'in play,' show up, transform, and reverse the systems which quietly order us about".[110]

The way a Narrative consultant enters into the discussion and conversation with organisations carves out the possibility of an alternative kind of relationship and connection that re-invites humanity back in every way. When an organisation is confronted with documentation and conversations around beliefs and ideas that are harmful and hurtful, it has the freedom to choose. So, even if organisations are entrenched in the limitations of the ground from which they grew, the unpredictability of our human narratives, knowledges, gifts and faith dares us to challenge and show up to live a counter-narrative.

THE WORK OF A NARRATIVE CONSULTANT

Applying a Narrative approach in the organisational development field employs the vital art of asking transformational questions, listening, documenting and creating a welcoming space (see chapter five). The skill of transformational listening and questioning serves as an invitation for all voices to participate and for all knowledges to be seen as valid in this participation.

---

109   Hancock, F & Epston, D. 2008. The Craft and Art of Narrative Inquiry in Organisations, p. 490.

110   Fillingham, L A 1993. *Foucault for Beginners*.

INVITATIONS TO BE UNMUTED

The artistry[111] of listening, questioning and documenting shows up in the practices of creating a space where everyone in the organisation

- feels free to speak
- is not judged or labelled
- offers words and meanings that are taken seriously without being "corrected" or replaced by the language of the consultant
- can speak freely about what matters to them
- is allowed to speak for him/herself.

Within the Narrative consulting approach the community of workers on all levels of the organisation is seen as knowledged and is invited to speak freely. This invitation challenges the assumption about who is allowed to speak, whose **"storied knowledges"**[112] are worth listening to, and what is regarded as acceptable to talk about. In the Narrative approach, consultants seek to bring to the fore the often disregarded, unnoticed or undervalued knowledges and stories of those considered and ranked as lower-level workers. In the story of hierarchy in the organisational world, the documentations of organisational knowledges and stories most often represent those at the senior executive or managerial levels. There is still a dominant belief that those at the top (CEO, senior executives and managers) of the organisation are the most important, know what is best for the organisation and will bring about real change. (This idea was explored and challenged in chapter 11.)

The Narrative work is committed to supporting minority voices, to magnifying the voice of so many who do not even know they have a voice. One way is to be a scribe, saying what employees are saying, the way the employees say it, in their voice, giving them a voice where before they had none. The silence of these voices is painful, and by writing down their words, by being their scribe, narrative practitioners are breaking the silence, becoming a voice for the voiceless, so that the silent ones can scream their story.

Participants in these Narrative processes appreciate the respect granted to them in the listening to and the documenting of their storied knowledges. The invitation to participate and the realisation that their contribution really matters form part of re-writing the dominant idea and belief that knowledges from the top levels are the only ones that really matter.

---

111 "Artistry" is an idea David Epston used at the Advanced Narrative Supervision workshop in Vancouver, in October 2011.

112 Hancock, F & Epston, D 2008. The Craft and Art of Narrative Inquiry in Organisations, p. 490.

INSIDER KNOWLEDGES AND LANGUAGE CONVEYED THROUGH STORIES

After the invitation has been extended to all levels of the work-community to speak freely, the consultant engages in respectful and inclusive practices of listening and asking questions that show s/he is open to being surprised and informed by the work-community. Even though the Narrative consultant's stance is that of someone who does not know all the answers, we bring the expertise of "knowing how to find things out."[113] These informed harvested knowledges that were discovered in the finding-out-journey can be called insider knowledges.

The following are examples of the kind of questions that can be asked:

*   *"If you were collectively to develop a story of how you worked together for the benefit of the community and for the long-term sustainability of the organisation, what organisational and individual practices would you need to avoid and what professional practices might you actively seek to reinforce and support each other to take up?*

*   *In reinforcing and taking up such chosen practices, are you also likely to grow trust and confidence in each other's the ability (board and management) to perform your particular roles in a professional manner?"*[114]

The conclusions that an organisation draws from the storied insider knowledges do not come from the know-it-all expertise of outside consultants. These stories come in the language of the people who work at all levels of the organisation, and reflect experiences that are known and lived.

COLLABORATING WITH THE ORGANISATION AS THE EXPERT

The Narrative approach does not impose answers, advice or new ideas on the challenges facing organisations. The community of workers is seen as the knowledgeable experts of their own narrative and they are treated as writers, painters and actors of their own book, canvas and drama.

Because the insider knowledges of an organisation are taken seriously, the stance of a narrative practitioner is to do things and find solutions *with* an organisation as an expert, participant and collaborator in the alternative narrative. When the client is viewed and treated as the expert, it requires a stance and practice that honours and respects the language, world and relationships of the client. The client is seen as resourceful, gifted and knowledgeable, with a storehouse of rich histories, values and competencies within a multiplicity of perspectives. Within this view, clients are the "authorities on their experience".[115]

---

113   Hancock, F & Epston, D 2008. The Craft and Art of Narrative Inquiry in Organisations, p. 490.

114   Hancock, F & Epston, D 2008. The Craft and Art of Narrative Inquiry in Organisations, p. 496.

115   Hancock, F & Epston, D 2008. The Craft and Art of Narrative Inquiry in Organisations, p. 496.

SEEING THE ORGANISATION AS SEPARATE FROM THE PROBLEM

At some point an organisation or community might experience being stuck. This can be the result of a traumatic event, a choice that the business/community made, a challenge that appears to be overwhelming, or may be related to outside factors over which they have no control. These moments in the life of an organisation or community can leave members in a place where they cannot see beyond the problem or challenge, or tap into new possibilities. The work of the Narrative consultant is to come alongside and enable the community or organisation to name the challenging or problem story in a language that is known to them, and to see themselves as separate from the problem story.

Narrative consultants are aware of the taken-for-granted beliefs and ideas that keep the problem story alive and they explore with the organisation how these ideas show up. Explorations are also undertaken in understanding who is authorised by the organisation to speak and who has the final say. The Narrative consultant is curious to explore the sometimes hidden alternative narratives that make their appearance within the journey.

The gift that this work brings is the outside ear that listens and a consultant who asks curious questions, so that those things that are taken for granted by the company are valued and seen anew. Externalising conversations invite the storied knowledges in an organisation to be seen as a social practice grounded in a rich history, legacy, manners and embodiment – all of which shows up in the organisational culture and managerial practices.[116] These knowledges are not deemed as belonging to or as privatised in the bodies of individuals or leaders in the organisation.

Again, the consultant does not decide for the organisation what the alternative narrative is, or what would be a good one to choose. The alternative possibilities to problem stories are already being lived and are already in use, but, because of the choice of whose voices are valued and heard in the organisation, they might just be hidden or taken for granted. The documentation and inquiry into the social practices and innovative ideas an organisation might take for granted give it public and formal recognition and acknowledgement. The organisation or community is the expert in this matter and makes its choices; the consultant acts as a scribe in documenting the choice and focus. These storied insider knowledges of the alternative narrative often do not fit into the grand scheme of things. The way forward is, therefore, in the work-community's hands and within their grasp, as these storied insider knowledges are already lived.

As a collaborator and participant in the chosen and owned alternative story, the Narrative consultant supports the alternative narrative by co-constructing rituals of celebration and by creating documents of identity. In addition, the consultant explores with the organisation the preferred community that will support the

---

116   Hancock, F & Epston, D 2008. The Craft and Art of Narrative Inquiry in Organisations, p. 493.

alternative narrative that is already on its way.[117] The expertise the consultant brings is to listen, to write and to facilitate the thickening and enriching of the alternative preferred story that has been named in experience-near language by the organisation.

THE GIFT OF THE NARRATIVE WORK TO ORGANISATIONS

The gifts of the Narrative work open up new worlds of possibility, healing, reconciliation and transformation, in a wide range of organisational development concerns – from teambuilding and conflict resolution, to strategic planning and executive coaching.

TRANSFORMING THE OTHER

The Narrative approach provides a space where we can tell our stories to one another. The beauty of our narratives is that there is nothing to argue about. They are the story and the meaning we have made of our lives, and therefore do not have to be explained or qualified.

When I present Narrative workshops in the US and Canada, some attendees do not want to tell their stories because they do not view them as coherent enough to be spoken out loud. Even before they are spoken, the stories are already judged and weighed in terms of importance and worthiness. In Africa and within black African cultures there is a deep respect for stories; for a story to be frowned upon or judged is indeed a foreign thought.

Witnessing one another's narratives provides the springboard for an alternative narrative, as we are no longer able to see the other within the confines of the language and taken-for-granted beliefs and ideas of our societies. Our own meanings are invited to shift as different stories enter and help us to move beyond our dominant problem stories about one another. We are able to move to a place where we can see anew and afresh that we are connected as human beings – as are our stories. As we enter one another's stories and allow them to transform our ideas and beliefs about one another, we are invited to choose again what we know and think about the other, as well as how we now want to live with one another.

Witnessing and participating in the stories of the other further transport us from the other and the stranger; we become neighbours. We are confronted with the other as mother, friend, child, family and neighbour. Therefore, a part of the new story in South Africa is a renewed respect for one another, not steeped in how we are different to the point where it makes us strangers. The alternative story creates a space where we can pause to see, from our common humanity, how different we are, yet how similar.

---

117 The preferred community is the group of community members whom the organisation selects; they can be clients of the organisation, local community members outside the community, leaders in the community, etc.

REDEEMING TIME

It was a cold August night in Limpopo province, and 20 South African souls were sitting around a fire, each wrapped in a blanket. I was the only white Afrikaner woman in the circle as we shared stories of the most important people in our lives and the incidents that most shaped our lives. Although the buses were waiting outside, they wanted to hear my story too. Being conscious that it was already late, I gave a brief, thin description of my life. Silence fell and one of the older men looked at me, shook his head and said in total surprise and disgust: "Did you fall from the sky?"

That night the penny dropped with regard to the different emphasis we place on our stories, and how we as Westerners want to brush over things, so dominated by what we have constructed as "time". It is as if we want to fast-track to intimacy and connectedness, without giving anything meaningful from our lives as a gift to the other – not even our time.

In black African culture, even greeting is an alternative story to speed and so-called efficiency. A greeting is not a hello or a goodbye; it is a story about your family and your home that unfolds. The pause in the greeting says we are connected; it is not seen as time-consuming, as the thought of people *not* pausing to see and be seen is unheard of. So often we hear, as white South African citizens, that we are rude because we do not greet. This greeting is more than the mere quick glance and uttering of a meaningless hello and goodbye; it is about redeeming the time and seeing our fellow human beings as such.

The Narrative work enables us to pause and live into the rhythm of the storytelling that cannot be rushed and pushed. As a result, the Narrative approach challenges ideas around speed and so-called effectiveness, as it joins hands with African culture in redeeming time as a gift to see, be touched by and connect with one another as human beings.

ENGAGING THE EMERGENT

Consulting in every organisation, community or nation means that we are aware of a rich history of challenges, relationships with problems and alternative narratives already emerging. To engage without an exploration of these narratives is to deny the gifts, genius and possibilities of an alternative future, and the rich history in which it is steeped.

Engaging with the problem stories of individuals or communities is not a search for what lies beneath, for who is to blame or for our weak points, so that we can be aware of or steer away from them. The exploration of the problem stories of a community or individual is an invitation to freedom and choice. It is a distancing from the known world, and sometimes the only world known. It is the languaging of what we have sometimes taken into our bodies and lives, and now have the opportunity to call out an alternative to.

In the Narrative work, the histories become an open mine for the possibilities of a community of individuals who rediscover their values, gifts and knowledges, and skills of living. Unique naming and metaphors of the histories open a rabbit hole of imaginative transformative possibility.

The gifts that the Narrative work brings to the organisational world are that it

- uses narratives in the process of discovery
- provides a space to speak about and challenge the harmful taken-for-granted beliefs and ideas of society
- taps into the rich histories of the stories of the world of work
- invites teams, groups and departments to see themselves as a community of workers, students, managers, etc.
- generates the buy-in of the work-community in terms of commitment and ownership of any organisational strategy, vision or initiative that flows from their knowledges and expertise
- asks the kinds of questions that invite people to participate as they gain something from the process
- invites the community of workers to re-write the organisational story as participants and actors in the organisational drama
- generates knowledges and narratives that are home-grown and owned in ways that can take the organisation forward
- thickens the alternative narrative.

These Narrative consultant practices can be applied in the areas of teambuilding, research, conflict management, diversity work, change processes, leadership development, strategic planning, debriefing and coaching. The invitation of these ideas to come and dance in the organisational arena is still in its infancy, but the Narrative practices willingly and eagerly long to participate in the co-construction of the story of *Abundance* with all work-communities.

PART V

THE TRANSFORMATIONAL NATURE OF THE NARRATIVE WORK

The philosophical approach that carries the practices in the Narrative work grows from an understanding that we construct our realities through our stories and relationships, and this invites the possibility of transformation to come alongside the work as a co-journeyer on the way.

The Narrative work provides a lens and practices that host and construct transformational conversations on an individual and communal level.

The final chapter of this book provides examples of the transformation that occurs as an outflow of these practices. In addition, the invitations to transformation as well as the nature of the transformational journey are explored.

CHAPTER THIRTEEN

INVITATIONS TO TRANSFORMATION

The Narrative work provides the non-threatening lens, language, approach and structure for transformation that propels us into creating a world that invites our humanity, gifts and communal connectedness with one another into our conversation. As we step into these portals of transformation in our co-constructing journeys, we are inviting whoever is in the room to be transformed as we transform our world together.

The *Oxford School Dictionary* defines "transformation" as the process of change of the "form or appearance or character of a person or a thing". After 13 years of journeying with the Narrative work in my own life and the lives of others, I know that these journeys facilitate more than just a mere change here and there. The form and appearance of individuals and communities undergo a complete turnaround – a change that spreads its tentacles into every aspect of their lives and worlds.

INVITATIONS AND PORTALS TO TRANSFORMATION

Whoever enters the Narrative journeys runs the risk of being transformed, because these practices, invitations and questions are all possible midwives to and agents for transformation. In part two, I proposed that the way narrative practitioners invite everybody in the room to participate when we come together is an invitation to

- re-humanise the world through the telling, re-telling and witnessing of the multiple stories of our lived experiences – stories we have interpreted and stories we are knowledgeable about
- re-name our world by giving our own language in the titles for our narratives
- re-authorise our world and lives by being aware of, challenging and resisting the taken-for-granted beliefs and ideas of people we authorise and hand the pen over to, in the writing of our lives
- re-dream a life, world and future through alternative narratives as we live into a different direction beyond what we have taken for granted
- re-communalise a world trapped in individualism and isolation, by allowing a community of co-journeyers to walk alongside
- re-gift our world by receiving and giving gifts abundantly, as we allow a community of co-journeyers to see and name what we are not always able to.

I propose that when we accept invitations to re-humanise, re-name, re-authorise, re-gift, re-communise and re-dream the worlds we live in, the world as we know it cannot but be transformed.

The Narrative work's invitations and portals to transformation are co-constructed in language, relationships, community and narrative. These co-constructions are created from and hosted in a warm, grace-filled, non-judgemental space, where the storyteller is listened to and can speak freely from his/her storied knowledges and gifts.

In listening fully, human beings are "seen into becoming", as the transformation of the dominant problem-saturated story moves into an alternative narrative that reconstructs their identity, meaning, agency, relationships and their worlds. This seeing in the listening brings an openness to relationships and the world that would previously never have been considered. These alternative relationships, possibilities and futures are indeed created from participants' deep connections to one another and to all things.

Transformation is also invited as the storyteller/community is treated as the one/group that can express and share storied knowledges and insights within their own words and language. This is especially relevant in a society where the voices of paid professionals and experts are valued and listened to the most. The invitation to participate, converse and think about our narratives in experience-near language opens up the possibility to see and understand so much more of the world than what can be grasped through the language of outsiders and experts. The transformational space in which participants are able to speak and validate their own experience in language they have "created" further frees them to voice. In the Narrative process a conversation that hosts all of the qualities mentioned above becomes the transformation that flows into the act of co-creating a preferred future, together with the insider knowledges in experience-near language.

The Narrative work provides the non-threatening lens, language, approach and structure for transformation that propel us into creating a world that invites our humanity, gifts and communal connectedness with one another as part of our conversation. As we step into these portals of transformation in our co-constructing journeys, we are inviting whoever is in the room to be transformed as we transform our world together.

Transformation is invited through examining the current story away from any person, team or community, in a space where the problem is the problem. The collaborative and participatory investigation and exploration of the current story and how it influences us give us the opportunity to again access our own voice, freedom and choice, in a world where the person is always labelled as the problem.

All of these invitations are carried by the transformational listening and questioning practices discussed in chapter five.

RE-AUTHORING AS A DOORWAY TO TRANSFORMATION

The Narrative way of being with communities, teams and organisations creates a safe space that invites everybody in the room to have a voice, to ask unsettling questions and to consider their own authorship and agency in the world. The transformational space for the story, the questions asked of the story, the respect for the language and the knowledges of the story, and the invitation to name the story in one's own words, metaphors and language, are very important steps in the invitations to re-authoring.

The storyteller is treated and questioned as the author of the story and as the expert in knowledge of the story. When a story is re-authored, everything transforms around and in it. Taking up the pen in re-writing the stories invites the storyteller back as author: the storyteller becomes more than a mere reciter of a familiar story of the way things are. The storyteller becomes a constructor of the worlds s/he lives in, no longer accepting of the way things are, but a participant and collaborator in re-authoring the world we live in. As Narrative work participants become authors they inevitably participate in the creation of a different world in which they have a transformative influence on everybody and everything with whom they interact. These re-authored stories and lives then flow into the transformation of the world, individuals, communities, organisations and nations.

THE MANIFESTATIONS OF TRANSFORMATION

The manifestations of transformation often enter in the most surprising, unexpected places and ways. Transformation can show up in

- the sparkle in people's eyes
- a healing of or relief in the body
- an embracing one's own humanity
- a point of no return to the old narrative
- a joy of being aware that amplifies every sense and experience
- a hope and faith that emerge
- a gratitude in celebrating community
- an awareness of an abundance of gifts.

These are only a few manifestations I have either witnessed or experienced in my own story's transformation, or the transformation of those I have been privileged to journey with. In this regard I agree with Rumi's observation that there are "as many ways through the opening of this transformation as there are human beings".[118]

---

118   Barks, C 2002. *The Soul of Rumi*... p. 19.

THE UNENDING TRANSFORMATION

In re-authoring our own stories, we embark on a never-ending journey of wonder and transformation.

In the rich tapestry of a multiplicity of narratives, our stories all dance together, continuously on the way to being made sense and meaning of. Our stories also are unfinished, as the transformative process of making new meaning will never take us to a place where we get everything right and are able to relax in an eternal status quo and bliss, proclaiming "This is my story now and for ever more". Even if we make this claim, invitations to reconsider, rethink and decide again are all around us, as sometimes irritating exceptions tug at the gift of our interpretive humanity.

Because our stories are always on the move as we make meaning, we can never slip back into the way things are – not even for our preferred stories. If we sit back and make claims that we are getting it right, now, finally, the preferred stories can also become stories that were once helpful but moved us back into the experience of being stuck. The multiplicity of realities and stories invites us into the dance of viewing our discoveries and the implications for our lives as being for the moment. In this flash of time and space, this is one of many preferred stories in my life. As we embrace this understanding, we begin to live a counter-story to the larger societal narrative with its quest to make truth claims of certainty and predictability, saying "This is my story, forever after".

It is important that participants invite a community of co-travellers who value and support the meaning they make of their preferred stories for now, to journey with them. This community then celebrates transformational moments with participants as they occur, and does not expect them to stay bound to one story and the singularity of that story.

This unending journey of transformation through the Narrative lens therefore gives us a view on the constant movement of our narratives, without having the motion be daunting. This lens has the grace to absorb the ebb and flow of our gifted and interpretive humanity. Our stories are on the move and they invite us to conversations that are never finished, complete or set in their meaning. Every story and every conversation becomes a springboard for the movement and transformation that might be waiting just around the corner.

THE SPACE IN-BETWEEN NARRATIVES

Given that our stories are on the move as we unpack them, we may, at times, be caught in the space in-between or in no-man's land between stories.[119] In this transition journey of repositioning, participants are occasionally trapped between two stories and the worlds they represent, as they continue their relationship

---

119 In this section the space in-between narratives is interchangeably called no-man's land, transition, or the wilderness journey. See Brueggemann, W 1999. The Liturgy of Abundance...

with both. Their relationship and connection to both stories result in participants dancing and moving between stories and worlds, as they sometimes choose to keep both stories alive.

Although we are constantly living in a multiplicity of narratives, there are times when the "end" has come, or a "re-negotiation" of a particular kind of relationship with a story is required. For some participants, the end of a problem-saturated story means that a choice has been made to thicken and engage in a more focused relationship with a chosen preferred alternative story. In this in-between space we should never underestimate the power of what participants are leaning into, once they have chosen to take up the pen and re-author their lives by writing and thickening their preferred narrative.

At times the wilderness journey is really tough, as the tentacles of the problem story are not content to let go too easily of their comfortable and predictable existence. This predictable existence has been constructed by the taken-for-granted ideas and beliefs in which problem stories are grounded. Transitioning out of a world that thinks it knows who the storytellers are and what they are about is surprising for all participants. The given or **taken-for-granted world** that participants are transitioning out of in a particular story, is always surprised when it no longer finds them willingly participating in the dance.

In the wilderness journey, the territory of the one whom the participants have authorised to speak is also revealed when the fiery balls of reprimand command them back into their "rightful place" (as a woman, man, spouse, employee, brother, sister, pastor, team, executive, leader). When these authorised voices discover that they are voiceless, de-authorised and have no effect, the given world groans and everyone again becomes unsure of the steps of this once-familiar dance.

The wilderness journey brings confusion and doubt as it takes time to complete the prior narrative. Problem stories are seldom dropped in an instant, as they are spied on and gradually folded into the fabric of our alternative preferred narrative. If participants announce that the problem story has been dropped and that everybody must make way for the alternative preferred narrative, it may be experienced as an act of violence towards the people with whom the participant journeys in his/her day-to-day living. Questions for narrative practitioners to consider include:

- *How do you then complete the problem narrative?*
- *How can you honour what came before, in addition to grieving over its death?*

Sometimes participants experience the uncertainty of the dance, grief and loss in the departure from and completion of the problem narrative. Participants might grieve for the suffering the relationship with this narrative has caused in their lives, and might lament how they compromised the values, hopes, dreams and gifts that are important to them. This can be a very painful journey.

These are some of the questions that we could ask ourselves and others when travelling in the wilderness or on stormy seas:

- *What are the incidents and events in this journey that keep you from drowning?*
- *What do you pay attention to in your transitional journey?*
- *What kinds of questions are you asking yourself on the way?*
- *How are your feet doing in this journey?*
- *When are the times or moments that you experience "an oasis"?*

As the relationship with the problem narrative shifts and changes, and the choice for the preferred future becomes clearer, participants face the futility of their efforts to still trust this narrative. For some, living with the dominant problem story is no longer an option, as they have been profoundly transformed by seeing a door that never closes. If the choice is to either let the problem narrative go or to live in a new relationship with this narrative, there are various ways to respectfully say goodbye. After all, at some stage in his/her life, the problem narrative served the storyteller well, and therefore respectful rituals of saying good-bye can and must be considered, for example:

- Organise a party for the old narrative in which it is thanked and celebrated for its contribution in the participant/community's life
- Create a ritual where the old narrative is sent off to help others along the way
- Sometimes the old narrative needs an individual or collective apology, given in the solidarity of a community that can bring healing and restoration.

When participants are faced with immense grief, searching for home, challenging the previously authorised voices and opening new territories of preferred stories, they may experience a feeling of being displaced, of social isolation and loneliness. Community is the answer to this storm of loneliness, pain and sadness. It is very important to allow participants time to sufficiently explore the naming of a preferred community that will walk this sometimes lonely road of being lost, grieving and wandering in the wilderness. Feeling loved and welcomed in the space in-between is the transportation from one world to the next, as it makes the feeling of being lost a little softer around the edges.

In addition, the loving preferred community walks alongside participants in enriching and thickening the alternative story, as it steps out of its baby shoes. When participants tell their story of becoming to the community, it does not have to be coherent or make sense. The mere openness in sharing what comes to the storyteller at that moment is taken as a gift. A community that welcomes participants with open arms and bodies, that has the time and space to embrace all of them, as is, is not a luxury but a necessity. These welcoming conversations are able to contain the frequency, intensity, richness and silence of the rhythm of life, and are gracious about human becoming. Making sense of what the storyteller is accepting, learning, realising and holding within a community of concern results in ultimate joy, and sometimes even relief. The journey with the community entails witnessing the learning, celebrating the alternative narrative, learning with participants, and seeing them in their human becoming. This collaboration with a community stands against the given culture which wants to render participants invisible in their becoming, and wants to make them obsolete.

In the journey through the wilderness, another possible participant in holding the space in-between is nature. The ocean, forests, deserts, rivers, waterfalls, mountains and gardens are all willing companions that are open to contain all of the complexity of the space in-between. When there is a conscious connection, nature also forms part of the community that understands and allows people to be as they are.

Through the poetry and the prose of our preferred narratives we can escape and challenge the thin descriptions that our society's taken-for-granted pretensions have in mind for us, as we collaboratively write alternative actions into life with our preferred community.

COMMUNAL TRANSFORMATION

We live in a time when communities desperately need to write a new and alternative communal narrative. The media bombard us with their advocacy for hopelessness and despair, as they offer us deficiency stories about communities, making us believe that they are the so-called watchdog and voice of a moral society. Being invited into the problem-saturated and thin description stories of communities only gives us more of the same, problem communities.

Narrative practitioners believe that communities are richly gifted with local wisdom and expertise, and that they just need to be provided with the space to reclaim, re-author and re-write their story. In harvesting the communal story, the Narrative approach provides useful and respectful readings and lenses of understanding that invite and include everyone as participants, in collectively making new meaning and creating a new future through conversations. Within these participatory collaborative processes, knowledge is not seen as something that one person has or does not have; knowledge is seen as a collaborative co-creating that people do together. The voices of all who enter and participate are welcomed and heard.

These collaborative spaces make it possible for communities to identify initiatives when they took action or are still taking action against problem stories. Therefore, Narrative practices want to work within an appreciative communal culture that richly describes the skills, gifts and knowledges which make them visible to the community and to others. This process includes tracing the history of these skills, knowledges and gifts. These ways of being are then linked to the local culture and to how they can strengthen these initiatives and live into the possibilities for them as a community.

In the Narrative work we have seen the close interrelatedness of the community's story with the individual narrative, and know that one cannot exist without the other; they are always linked. Our life stories are informed by the communities we live in, and our communal narrative is informed by the individual life stories that respond to and act on the communal narrative. We also know that something profound happens at the intersection of the communal and the individual story that forms the seeds of transformation.

Wilfred Draft uses the compelling image of the sea to explain how the whitecaps in the ocean represent leaders of an organisation.[120] He explains that in the end, the deep blue sea of members of an organisation or community of workers determines the direction and capabilities of the ocean. The whitecaps crash and vanish into the sea. The respectful dance between the whitecaps and the deep blue sea of ordinary people will determine the direction, turn the tide and witness how the deep blue sea can bring transformation into its daily tidal rhythm. The community, the collective, as the ripples of the ordinary people in the sea of life, will change the entire surface of the ocean while it changes as it moves and continues to move.

TRANSFORMATION OF ALL THAT WE HAVE KNOWN

The world we live in is constructed by the meaning we have made in language and by the relationships in which we stand. This constructed world is supported by the taken-for-granted beliefs and ideas which are accepted by a particular society and culture, and the people we have authorised to speak. Our transformed narratives re-author these constructed worlds as the ripple effect demands a response, a reaction, an engagement or a celebration. The ripple effect of the narrative of an individual or community's transformation has implications for all the relationships, beliefs, ideas and possibilities in which they stand. As a result, the transformed narrative touches everyone: those who wish for things to stay the same, those who have shouted a grief cry for things to change, and those who thought things were just fine.

When the possibility of an alternative or counter-narrative is named, explored and lived, the world is not always happy; it may be a bit unsure and unsettled, or even angry. On the other hand, the world around the community and individual might have been groaning and waiting, ready for the transformation, ready to come alongside the alternative narrative and ready live it with them. When the narrative of a community or individual has transformed into the preferred/alternative/counter-story, those different worlds will have different reactions to the ripple effect.

A WORLD THAT IS READY TO LEAP INTO THE TRANSFORMED NARRATIVE

Sometimes the community is excited and curious about the transformation it is witnessing. Its members may even have been longing for the transformation in their own lives and may be ready to be transformed when they witness the possibility of transformation showing up in other people's lives and stories. The stories of Meshach and Martin, participants in the Personal Change Programme workshops at AngloAmerican Platinum, exemplify such stories of acceptance and wonder about the transformation of their narratives.[121]

---

120   Draft, W 2001. *The Deep Blue Sea*....

121   The stories of Meshach and Martin are included here with their permission.

Meshach found his manager and family fully embracing the transformed narrative of his life. After the workshop had created a space for Meshach's story of work to be transformed, he no longer felt the need to challenge and question his manager. In addition, he no longer lost his temper or shouted in the workplace. His curious manager asked him what they had "given" him at the workshop, because he could plainly see the transformation. Meshach's family also experienced the transformation as respect entered their home. He no longer dismissed his children and his wife, saying that he had paid *lobola* for her.[122] When there were things to discuss, he now spoke to his wife first, and then they spoke to the children together. Now Meshach sees his children differently, no longer as only having to be obedient and respectful to him. He includes them in family matters when changes have to be made. One of the changes the children requested was that he bring the water pipe closer to the house, so that the children wouldn't have to walk so far to fetch water before school. He explained that the children are now happier, as is his wife, and they wanted to know what had brought about this transformation.

Martin also explained how his life was transformed after the workshop. He now takes the time to see his extended family regularly and is becoming aware of serious problems that he did not even know about. He now organises family meetings once or twice a year so the family's relatives can get to know one another better. He has a dream that no child in his family will be uneducated, and is making that dream come true for all the children in the family. One of the company values, "we are one team", has become how Martin sees his own family. This transformed story had Martin's family asking whether there is something wrong with him, because he wants to be with them so regularly now.

Whoever is witnessing and celebrating such transformations (as did the manager and families in Meshach's and Martin's stories) joins the community of concern, as their curiosity and celebration further thicken and enrich the alternative narrative of becoming.

WHEN THE WORLD FROWNS AND LONGS FOR THINGS AS THEY WERE

There is a part of the world we live in that is complacent about the way things are – a world that has settled into the status quo of life. In its acceptance of complacency, it will never be ready for the transformed narrative. This might be because those individuals or groups benefit from the way things are, and deep down are not interested in things really transforming. Transforming this accepted world would mean that life as they know it, and which they benefit from, will change and then they will have to change as well.

---

122 *Lobolo* or *lobola* in Zulu, Xhosa and Ndebele (*mahadi* in Sesotho, *roora* in Shona and *magadi* in Northern Sotho), sometimes translated as bride price, is a traditional southern African custom whereby the man pays the family of his fiancée for her hand in marriage. (Compare with the European dowry custom, where the woman brings assets.) The custom is aimed at bringing two families together, fostering mutual respect, and indicating that the man is capable of supporting his wife financially. See: http://en.wikipedia.org/wiki/Lobolo

An example of how we as human beings have settled into the way things are, is the fact that we in the Western world have accepted that some people have food to eat while others do not. This means that there are people on this planet who go to bed hungry every day, and some even die of hunger. The alternative voice, question and story dare to ask: If we have an economic system that serves the people, and not the other way around, surely everyone on this planet will be able to eat and can continue to live in this life, right now.[123] Our acceptance of the current economic narrative is an example of how we have, over time, grown accustomed to the world that surrounds us, and have grown used to living in a particular way. We might not even like the world we live in, and we may have tried to challenge the way things are, but we have given up and accepted life as it is. Given our complacency about the way things are, the world is seldom ready for what is about to happen when known and familiar narratives are transformed, even if it is for the common good.[124]

An example of the un-readiness of the given world, in terms of a CEO's alternative preferred narrative, showed up in the shipping industry.[125] A certain CEO intentionally decided to pay his receptionists more than the industry going rate, because he values the work they do as a first point of contact with clients of the company. This alternative narrative has caused all kinds of ripple effects in the industry and in people's lives: the husband of one receptionist asked her to resign because she now earns more than he does, and other CEOs phoned to say that the CEO was causing havoc in the industry, by paying his receptionists so well. The CEO has disregarded the white noise of the given world, with its taken-for-granted beliefs and ideas about what receptionists are "worth" in monetary terms, and as a result his world has been transformed, both willingly and unwillingly. The alternative narrative becomes an indictment and challenge to every individual, team or community it stands in relationship to. Their given worlds, and the smallness of the scarcity that people have tended to accept as the way things are, are now up for grabs.

But how do we engage with a world that wants to stay the same? What are the tasks and responsibilities of the individuals and communities living into the alternative/counter or preferred narrative?

Engaging in Narrative conversations is a risky business, as lives, relationships and contexts transform because of it – this can be frightening for some. The process of reconstructing and negotiating our own identities is therefore often conflict-ridden, because not everybody whose life is affected by the transformation is willing to have the conversation. It is the easiest thing to revert back to the language and world which people know, and the person whose narrative has been transformed is sometimes served with a new label such as "bitch", "feminist", "selfish", "idealist", "dreamer", "arrogant", and the like. The old naming is often merely replaced with new labels that close down the conversation.

123   Saunders, O Forthcoming. *Shifting the Economics.*

124   Brueggemann, W 2010. *Journey to the Common Good.*

125   As told to me by Olivia Saunders.

Participants sometimes live in the paradox of a growing alternative narrative against the backdrop of the dissonance of a larger or specific narrative that does not wish to be tainted or touched by the movement of the individual or communal narrative. This attitude on the part of the given world leaves people with no choice but to live within the paradox and ambiguity of this multiplicity of narratives.

Although we know that the world and relationships we enter into are mostly not interested in a conversation around the transformed narrative, we have a responsibility to at least have the conversation, where possible. Chapter five provides excellent guidelines for a conversation that invites people to say the unspeakable and to talk about it away from the person as the problem. I would, however, highlight a few of the guidelines that pertain particularly to these kinds of conversations.

It is very important to remain respectful and gracious without assuming or judging the person or group that acts with surprise, disillusionment and even irritation, as they long for the predictability of the old story to return. It is of the utmost importance that we are never so sure about our preferred stories that we cannot be curious about how the transformed narrative is influencing others, and why the relationship matters so much to them.

In the light of the paradox and the frequent unwillingness of the given world to have a conversation around the transformed narrative, the preferred community's concern and support for this narrative being lived and richly described are very important. The characteristic loneliness and the feeling of being lost – even thoughts that surely you want too much or that you are going mad – can be countered by the community journeying with the participant. When participants engage with people or groups that are not supportive of the chosen, preferred stories, participants' close connections to their community of concern will provide them with the documents of identity needed to open a world in which both doubt and questions can be explored. The survival of the alternative preferred story is grounded in new identity conclusions, supported by the community concerned, in the unfolding of this new alternative narrative.

Infinite stars from which to make a pattern.

Patterning a story

that is ours to make.

Even across vast distance

we connect the space between.

The inward story

and the outer pattern

reflect

perfectly.

Arising concurrently

in our transformation

– Ward Mailliard[126]

The Narrative approach offers a lens not only to make sense of the infinite stars of our life's narratives, but to transform the making of the patterns in the sky of our lives and communities. Re-authoring our world occurs through the transformation of one individual and communal narrative or one living autobiography at a time. As we re-author the worlds we live in, we are engaging with transformation as the "slow, steady process of inviting each other into a counter-story about God, world, neighbour and self".[127] At some point in our human connectedness, our transformed narratives will join, arise concurrently, and forever change and re-author the planet's dominant story of isolation, greed, scarcity, abuse and violence, into an alternative counter-narrative of . . .

---

126   Ward Mailliard is a brilliant teacher who co-constructs learning journeys with students at Mount Madonna School on a daily basis. See: http://mountmadonnaschool.org/values/

127   Brueggemann, W 1993. *Text Under Negotiation...*

READING LIST FOR THE CURIOUS

As promised, below is a list of reading material I recommend if you are interested in finding out more.

WEBSITES

If you enjoy browsing and exploring, you can consult the following websites that will keep you informed of the latest conferences and training events, as well as numerous free articles which are posted online.

http://www.dulwichcentre.com.au/

http://www.facebook.com/groups/269945769703564/ (The tree of life as methodology for the Narrative approach)

http://therapeuticconversations.com/

http://www.narrativeapproaches.com/

http://www.narrativetherapychicago.com/

BOOKS

These books were very important in my training as a Narrative therapist and I still refer to them and re-read them. In the list you will also find books I recently discovered that inform my practice.

Denborough, D. 2008. *Collective Narrative Practice: Responding to Individuals, Groups and Communities Who have Experienced Trauma*. Adelaide, Australia: Dulwich Centre Publications.

Freedman, J & Combs, G. 1996. *Narrative Therapy: The Social Construction of Preferred Realities*. New York: Norton.

Hancocks, F & Epston, D. 2008. The Craft and Art of Narrative Inquiry in Organisations, in Barry, D & Hansen, H, *The Sage Handbook of New Approaches to Organisation Studies*, 485–502. London: SAGE Publications Ltd.

Kotzé, D, Myburg, J, Roux, J & Associates. 2002. *Ethical Ways of Being*. Pretoria: Ethics Alive.

Kotzé, E & Kotzé, D. 2001. Telling Narratives, Doing Spirituality, in Kotzé, E & Kotzé, D (eds), *Telling Narratives*, 1–14. Spellbound edition. Pretoria: Ethics Alive.

Madigan, S & Law, I (eds). 1998. *Praxis*. Vancouver: Yaletown Family Therapy.

Morgan, A. 2000. *What is Narrative Therapy*? Adelaide: Dulwich Centre Publications.

White, M. 2004. *Narrative Practice and Exotic Lives: Resurrecting Diversity in Everyday Life*. Adelaide: Dulwich Centre Publications.

White, M & Epston, D. 1990. *Narrative Means to Therapeutic Ends*. New York: Norton.

WORKS CONSULTED

Anderson, H. 1997. *Conversation, Language, and Possibilities: A Postmodern Approach to Therapy*. New York: Basic Books.

Anderson, H & Goolishian, H. 1988. Human Systems as Linguistic Systems: Preliminary and Evolving Ideas about the Implications for Clinical Theory. *Family Process* 27(4), 371–393.

Anderson, H & Goolishian, H. 1992. The Client is the Expert: A Not-knowing Approach to Therapy, in McNamee, S & Gergen, K J (eds), *Therapy as Social Construction*, 25–39. London: Sage.

Appignanesi, R & Garratt, C. 2003. *Introducing Postmodernism*. Duxford: Icon.

Barks, C. 2002. *The Soul of Rumi: A New Collection of Ecstatic Poems*. San Francisco: HarperCollins Publishers.

Block, P. 2008. *Community: The Structure of Belonging*. San Francisco: Berrett-Koehler Publishers.

Block, P & McKnight J. 2010. *The Abundant Community: Awakening the Power of Families and Neighbourhoods*. San Francisco: Berrett-Koehler.

Brueggemann, W. 1993. *Text Under Negotiation: The Bible and Postmodern Imagination*. Minneapolis: Fortress.

Brueggemann, W 1999. The Liturgy of Abundance, The Myth of Scarcity. *The Christian Century* (March 24–31): 342–347.

Brueggemann, W. 2010. *Journey to the Common Good*. Westminster: John Knox Press.

Burr, V. 1995. *An Introduction to Social Constructionism*. London: Routledge.

Denborough, D. 2008. *Collective Narrative Practice: Responding to Individuals, Groups and Communities Who have experienced Trauma*. Adelaide, Australia: Dulwich Centre Publications.

Doan, R E. 1998. The King is Dead; Long Live the King: Narrative Therapy and Practicing what we Preach. *Family Process* 37(3), 379–385.

Draft, W. 2001. *The Deep Blue Sea: Rethinking the Source of Leadership*. San Francisco: Jossey-Bass.

Epston, D. 2002. Presentation at a Workshop in Pretoria 10, 12–13 August.

Epston, D. 2011. Advanced Supervision Workshop in Vancouver, 20–23 October 2011.

Fillingham, L A. 1993. *Foucault for Beginners*. New York: Writers and Readers.

Foucault, M. 1977. *Discipline and Punish*. London: Penguin.

Foucault, M. 1980. *Power/Knowledge: Selected Interviews and Other Writings, 1972–1977*, ed and tr by C Gordon. New York: Pantheon.

Freedman, J & Combs, G. 1996. *Narrative Therapy: The Social Construction of Preferred Realities*. New York: Norton.

Freire, P. 1993. *Pedagogy of the Oppressed*. New revised 20th-anniversary edition. Tr by M B Ramos. New York: Continuum.

Freire, P. 1994. *Pedagogy of Hope: Reliving "Pedagogy of the Oppressed"*. Tr by R R Barr. New York: Continuum.

Geertz, C. 1973. Thick Description: Toward an Interpretive Theory of Culture, in Geertz, C., *The Interpretation of Cultures*. New York: Basic Books.

Gergen, K J. 1991. *The Saturated Self: Dilemmas of Identity in Contemporary Life*. New York: Basic Books.

Gergen, K J. 1994. *Realities and Relationships: Soundings in Social Construction*. Cambridge, Massachusetts: Harvard University Press.

Gergen, M & Gergen, K J (eds). 2003. *Social Construction: A Reader*. London: Sage.

Inchausti, R. 1991. The Ignorant Perfection of Ordinary People. Albany, NY: State University of New York Press.

Hancock, F & Epston, D. 2008. The Craft and Art of Narrative Inquiry in Organisations, in Barry, D and Hansen, H., *The Sage Handbook of New Approaches to Organisation Studies*, 485–502. London: Sage Publications Ltd.

Heshusius, L. 1994. Freeing Ourselves from Objectivity: Managing Subjectivity or Turning Toward a Participatory Mode of Consciousness? *Educational Researcher* 23(3), 15–22.

Hoffman, L. 1990. Constructing Realities: An Art of Lenses. *Family Process* 29(1), 1–12.

http://www.blogtalkradio.com/robert_thompson/2012/03/05/robert-thompsons-thought-grenades

http://therapeuticconversations.com/tcxconference/tcx-handouts/

http://www.abundantcommunity.com/home/posts/peter_block/parms/1/post/20110525_the_economics_of_neighborliness.html

http://www.dulwichcentre.com.au/what-is-narrative-therapy.html

http://www.narrativeapproaches.com/Book%20Folder/Down%20Under%20Up%20Over/DE_UO_111–192.pdf

http://www.narrativeapproaches.com/narrative%20papers%20folder/white_interview.htmhttp://www.narrativeapproaches.com/narrative%20papers%20folder/white_interview.htm

http://nearemmaus.com/2011/08/06/walter-brueggemann-interviewed-by-krista-tippett/

http://www.peterblock.com/_assets/downloads/Converse8%20Peter%20Block.pdf

http://www.yesmagazine.org/issues/what-happy-families-know/the-good-life-its-close-to-home

http://www.youtube.com/watch?v=HUoZuEnoEkk&feature=youtu.be

Johnson, A. 2005. *The Gender Knot: Unraveling Our Patriarchal Legacy*, 2nd ed. Philadelphia: Temple University Press.

Kotzé, D. 2002. Doing Participatory Ethics, in Kotzé, D, Myburg, J, Roux, J & Associates, *Ethical Ways of Being*, 1–34. Pretoria: Ethics Alive.

Kotzé, E & Kotzé D J. 1997. Social Construction as a Postmodern Discourse: An Epistemology for Conversational Therapeutic Practice. *Acta Theologica* 17(1), 27–50.

Lindemann Nelson, H. 2001. *Damaged Identities, Narrative Repair*. Ithaca, NY: Cornell University Press.

Madigan, S. 1998. The Politics of Identity: Locating Community Discourse in Narrative Practice, in Madigan, S & Law, I (eds), *Praxis: Situating Discourse, Feminism and Politics in Narrative Therapies*, 81–108. Vancouver: Yaletown Family Therapy.

Madigan, S. 2010. Notes on Workshop at the 9th Narrative Therapeutic Conversations, Madigan S & Epston, D. 1998. From 'Spy-chiatric Gaze' to Communities of Concern'; From Professional monologue to Dialogue, in Epston, D. ttp://therapeuticconversations.com

Madigan, S & Law, I (eds). 1998. *Praxis: Situating Discourse, Feminism and Politics in Narrative Therapies*. Vancouver: Yaletown Family Therapy.

Mailliard, W. 2010. Chautauqua, Mount Madonna School. July 2010.

McMinn, M R & Phillips, T R (eds). 2001. *Care for the Soul: Exploring the Intersection of Psychology and Theology*. Downers Grove, Illinois: InterVarsity Press.

McNamee, S & Gergen, K J (eds). 1992. *Therapy as Social Construction*. London: Sage.

Min, A K. 2004. *The Solidarity of Others in a Divided World: A Postmodern Theology after Postmodernism*. Madison Square Park, NY: T & T Clark.

Morgan, A. 2000. *What is Narrative Therapy? An Easy to Read Introduction*. Adelaide: Dulwich Centre.

Sampson, E E. 1989. The Deconstruction of the Self, in Shotter, I & Gerkin, K J (eds), *Texts of Identity*, 1–19. London: Sage.

Saunders, O. 2013. 'Shifting the Economics,' adapted from forthcoming book by the same title and used by permission.

Sween, E. 1998. The One Minute Question: What is Narrative Therapy? Some Working Answers. *Gecko* 12, 3–6.

White, M. 1988/89. The Externalizing of the Problem and the Re-authoring of Lives and Relationships. *Dulwich Centre Newsletter* Summer (special edition). Republished 1989 in White, M: *Selected Papers*, 5–28. Adelaide, Australia: Dulwich Centre Publications.

White, M. 1991. Deconstruction and Therapy. *Dulwich Centre Newsletter* 3, 21–40.

White, M. 1995. *Re-authoring Lives: Interviews and Essays*. Adelaide: Dulwich Centre.

White, M. 1997. *Narratives of Therapists' Lives*. Adelaide: Dulwich Centre.

White, M. 2001a. Narrative Practice and the Unpacking of Identity Conclusions. *Gecko: A Journal of Deconstruction and Narrative Ideas in Therapeutic Practice* (1), 28–55.

White, M. 2001b. Narrative Practice and the Unpacking of Identity Conclusions. http://www.psybc.com/pdfs/library/WHITE.pdf

White, M. 2003. Narrative Therapy and Externalizing the Problem, in Gergen, M & Gergen, K J (eds), *Social Construction: A Reader*, 163–168. London: Sage.

White, M. 2004a. Folk Psychology and Narrative Practices, in Angus, L E & McLeod, J (eds), *The Handbook of Narrative and Psychotherapy: Practice, Theory and Research*, 15–52. Thousand Oaks, California: Sage.

White, M. 2004b. *Narrative Practice and Exotic Lives: Resurrecting Diversity in Everyday Life*. Adelaide: Dulwich Centre Publications

White, M & Epston, D. 1990. *Narrative Means to Therapeutic Ends*. New York: Norton.

Winslade, J. 2009. Tracing Lines of Flight: Implications of the Work of Gilles Deleuze for Narrative Practice. *Family Process* 48, 332–346.

Wittgenstein, L. 1922. *Tractatus, Logico-Philosophicus*. New York: Harcourt Brace.

Wittgenstein, L. 1953/2001. *Philosophical Investigations*. Oxford: Blackwell Publishing.

Working with the Stories of Women's Lives. 2001. Ed by the Dulwich Centre. Adelaide: Dulwich Centre.

Wylie, M S. 1994. Panning for Gold. *Family Therapy Networker* 18(6), 40–48.

GLOSSARY

alternative narrative or **alternative story** – alternative narratives or stories grow from the **rich description** of **knowledges**, gifts, skills, hopes, dreams, histories and relationships of the **preferred narratives** of an individual or community's lives.

community of concern – a group of people whom an individual or community has chosen to come alongside them in their journey of living into an **alternative story** for their lives.

community of workers – in the Narrative consulting approach, the client or organisation is viewed as a **community of workers** or **work-communities** (also known as the workforce). This description talks about and to the idea that not only do people come to work, produce, serve and ensure profit, but they are a community of human beings who are working together to make a living and co-create a working environment, in line with their values, hopes and dreams for the future. On all levels, **communities of workers** are seen as key informants and contributors to what is known and can be known in the future (also known as the vision) of the organisation.

constructed narrative – we are not mere recipients of the **narratives** of our lives. We construct narratives by gathering evidence and incidents over many years, and organising them into the themes of our lives through the meaning we make of them. The construction of **narratives** is an active process as we negotiate our **narratives** within communities or societies, and in our culture.

constructed story – see **constructed narrative**

counterstory – a **counterstory** is a **narrative** that is counter/an alternative or other than the dominant story from which a person sometimes draws his/her identity. For example, if a person believes that s/he is not loveable, a **counterstory** will present evidence and incidents of times when Not Loveable was not all there was, to the story of that person's life.

counter-narrative – see **counterstory.**

counter-files – see **counterstory.**

documentalist – the narrative practitioner is a scribe or **documentalist** of the narratives, histories, gifts and knowledges of the people s/he journeys with. A documentalist writes documents that richly describe a **counterstory** which serves as a springboard for the dreams and hopes of **storytellers**. This documentation is written in the language and words of the **storytellers**, within the process of the Narrative work.

documents of identity – these are rich narratives and descriptions of the skills, gifts, knowledges and relationships of participants, that can be presented in the form of letters, songs, certificates, notes, poems, art, photos, etc. These documents support and thicken the **alternative narrative.**

dominant problem narrative – these are stories that have convinced human beings to live according to thin **identity conclusions** that are limiting to their preferred way of doing and being in this world.

dominant problem-saturated narratives – a **narrative** in which the person is seen as the problem, the reason for the problem, and the cause of the problem. These kinds of **narratives** reflect that the problem is all there is to the person; the problem-saturated narrative becomes the only story possible about the person.

experience-near – this kind of talk is reflected in expressions, experiences and descriptions in our own words, as we make meaning of what is familiar to us and what we have named. It means that no one else has imposed their language, descriptions or ideas on us, but we have spoken from our experience, history and **knowledges** in a way that makes sense to how we think and what we believe about the world.

experience-near description – see **experience-near.**

expert – in the Narrative work we see the **storyteller** as the **expert** of the stories of his/her life. The **listener** in the Narrative work asks questions of the **storyteller** as the **expert**, meaning that s/he holds the multiplicity of stories, **knowledges**, values, hopes and dreams of his/her preferred life.

externalisation – this is an approach that helps us to speak and be with individuals or communities in ways in which they are seen as separate from the problem stories that inform their lives.

externalising language – this is a way of speaking and a stance of listening where the person is not the problem and the problem is not inside the person. When a **storyteller** says: "I am fearful," the narrative practitioner will ask: "When did Fearful first enter your life?" This way of speaking always separates the person from the problem, and takes the problem outside of the person, by using **externalised language**.

gifts – when listening to a storyteller, narrative practitioners are always aware that they are not only witnessing a story, but in the listening their lives are also touched by the story of the other. This point, of being moved or touched by the stories being listened to, I have come to call **gifts**. Gifts can be learnings from a story, a reminder of my own values and beliefs which I may have forgotten, a challenge to my own beliefs and ideas about something, an experience of not being alone in my own struggles and thoughts, and so forth.

given world – we have come to understand this as the way things are. We often hear the expression that this or that is a given, meaning that it cannot be changed or challenged.

identity conclusions – because humans are interpreting beings, actions and events are taken into a **meaning-making** process, and from that **participants** draw conclusions about who they are and what they can become.

insider knowledges – David Epston explains that **insider knowledges** have the following qualities: they are "local, particular and at times unique as they often arise from imagination and inspiration, not the usual technologies of scientific knowledge-making. ... Because they are, in the first instance, the intellectual property or otherwise of the person(s) concerned, outsiders cannot rightly claim either invention or ownership of such **knowledges**. '**Insider knowledges**' are modest and make no claims beyond the person(s) concerned. They do not seek any monopolies of "knowing", but sponsor many kinds and ways of knowing. '**Insider knowledges**' do not provide grand schemes as they are far too humble for that ... and are carried best by and through stories."

internalised self-surveillance – this is the practice by which an individual (or a community) constantly weighs and measures him/herself in terms of their interpretation of societal values, beliefs and ideas. Not only are they subject to the surveillance of the communities and families within which those individuals live, but they take this surveillance inside their life and body, and start to judge, measure and compare themselves in what we call **internalised self-surveillance**.

knowledges – the word refers to the multiplicity of **knowledges** that an individual, community or organisation has in the art and skill of living their lives in this world.

landscape of action questions – these questions invite people to notice actions and intentions that contradict or deny the dominant problem story, and to describe and expand on them in detail. These questions ask: Who? What? When?

landscape of identity questions – these questions, which assist with the process of thickening and enriching **unique outcomes**, can be situated in the past, present and future. The storyteller is invited to reflect on the meaning of the events s/he has described. The landscape of identity asks questions about the why: What does this mean to you and why does it matter?

listener – a listener is a person who uses the Narrative practices as a lens to listen to, and be curious about, the stories of individuals, coachees, teams, communities or organisations.

local or insider knowledges – these are **knowledges** and expertise built on the lived experiences and actions of human beings. They are local because they grow from the communities in which people live, and they are "insider" because people living the life are speaking from the **knowledges** of their lived experiences.

meaning making – humans are interpreting beings who cannot but make meaning of their lives. The conclusions human beings draw about their identity are therefore the end product of a **meaning-making** process that occurs in relationships, in communities and cultural life, and within understandings.

narrative – a string of incidents and events that took place over a period of time, and which human beings have made meaning of in a way that influences their actions, identity conclusions and possibilities for the future.

ordinary people – those people who are not named by their title, their role in society or the power they hold, i.e. they are everyday people.

other – this refers to any person who is different from me in any way in terms of race, gender, educational level, age, culture, economic status, etc.

participant – the Narrative practices work from the idea that we journey together and co-participate in the conversation and the re-writing of our stories. Therefore, a "participant" can refer to workshop participants, but mostly it describes the **storytellers** and listeners in the Narrative process.

preferred community – these are community members whom the individual or organisation selects to journey alongside them, in order to thicken the **alternative story**. The **preferred community** can consist of clients of the organisation, local community members outside the community, leaders in the community, etc. See also **community of concern.**

problem stories – these are stories that lead to thin conclusions about a person/team/community's identity. **Problem stories** do not tell the whole story, or richly describe the story. Such stories have real effects on people's lives and identities, and often people feel stuck and trapped by them.

re-author – when an individual or a community takes back the pen in the active participation and writing as authors of their lives, they are re-authoring their lives in alternative, preferred ways that grow from their gifts, skills, values, hopes and dreams.

self-surveillance – see **internalised self-surveillance.**

societal ideas and beliefs – see **taken-for-granted ideas and beliefs.**

sparkling event – see **unique outcome.**

spy/spying on the problem story – this means that we are aware of the story, how it shows up, when it shows up, how it invites us to pay attention to it, and what kind of tactics it employs to make us believe it is the only story that is real or true.

statement of position – after an individual (or community) is asked to describe his/her life in a rich/thick way, s/he is invited to state the position s/he now wants to take on that story.

storied knowledges – these are the **knowledges** of **storytellers** that are told and/or documented through the stories they tell. Such **knowledges** are carried by and through stories, while the stories carry people's **knowledges**.

storyteller – a **storyteller** could be any individual, coachee, community, team or organisation that consults a narrative practitioner about the meaning they have attributed to the different stories of their lives.

stranger – see **other.**

taken-for-granted ideas and beliefs – these ideas and beliefs (also known as societal discourses) have survived over a long period of time in a culture, community and organisation, in such a way that they become the way things are or have always been done. They are never questioned or challenged.

taken-for-granted world – see **given world**.

tentacles of the problem story – problem stories stand in a relationship with the **storyteller**, and sometimes have a long legacy of influences and interactions with that storyteller. **Tentacles** is a metaphor for describing how problem stories make themselves at home. The narrative practitioner's work is to ask questions to and about the reach of the **problem story** in the life and relationships of the **storyteller**.

the other – see **other**.

thick/rich description – these descriptions value the multiplicity of a person/community's life stories and link these stories to the history and multiplicity of relationships in which they stand. For example, I am an Afrikaner, theologian, consultant, facilitator and musician, who engages with individuals, communities and organisations in ways that co-construct transformation in this world.

thin description – this is when individuals or communities talk about themselves, a situation or another person, in a way that only values a singular story that makes the claim of truth for all times and in all ways. For example, white Afrikaners are racist.

totalise – the sum total of people's identities is wrapped up in totalising statements, which are regarded as the only and all-encompassing label or identity of a person, community or organisation.

truth claims – in society, certain ideas and beliefs have attained the status of truths. These **truth claims** are very powerful, as nobody can defend themselves against them, challenge them or ask them questions. Not only are they frequently referred to as "the way it is", but these truths are also advocated by people in society whose voices are valued and acknowledged as the conveyers of the truth, and as the ones who know the truth. These **truth claims** are spoken about as universal, meaning that they are always true for everybody, in every culture, society and community, at any given time.

unique outcome – every moment that looks different from the problem story is called a **unique outcome** or a **sparkling event**. **Unique outcomes** are incidents in the past or present where people had some influence over the problem and experienced themselves as free or distant from the problem story. These unique experiences form pockets of light for an alternative preferred story. The **unique outcome** may be a plan, action (sometimes just showing up for a conversation is an alternative future), feeling, statement, quality, desire, dream, thought, belief, ability or commitment. Whenever the telling or re-telling of the **unique outcome** or **sparkling event** is witnessed, the person looks physically different: their eyes sparkle, and they pause as they enter the possibility and remembering of this story.

unlisted language – in an interview titled 'Aliveness and the Timeless Way of Helping', Lynn Hoffman introduces the idea of **unlisted** or hidden language which exists, but has not been qualified as a proper subject deserving of description. In the same way, people make meaning of their lives and name the stories they live by in language that might not be acknowledged or qualified as "proper". **Unlisted language** therefore opens up the possibility for the world to be named in a new and unlisted way.

work-community or **work-communities** – Pierre Blanc-Sahnoun introduced me to the idea of speaking about the workforce as **work-communities**, which opens up much richer descriptions and possibilities. I use the terms **work-communities** and **community of workers** interchangeably.

ABOUT THE AUTHOR

 **Chené Swart** is a writer, speaker and consultant for Transformations, a consulting company that provides services to small, medium and large businesses, communities, and educational institutions in South Africa, the US, Canada and the Bahamas. The company has been providing leadership development, training, diversity journeys, coaching, research, facilitation and consulting services to a diverse range of clients over the past eight years.

In her work as an executive and life coach, consultant and trainer in Narrative practices, Chené co-creates transformational learning contexts and journeys. She invites and enables participants to re-write and re-author the stories of their lives as individuals, communities and organisations where they feel stuck or trapped or where the stories they continuously tell are thin conclusions that do not honour the gifts, values and knowledges of these groups or individuals. These individual, communal and organisational alternative narratives open the possibility to write and live into a new preferred future. The key outcomes of these participative journeys are personal and communal agency, new ways of doing and being, and transformed lives.

Through Transformations, Chené offers various workshops that apply Narrative practices in the contexts of leadership, stress management, consultancy, coaching, diversity work, empowerment, conflict resolution, transformation processes and teambuilding. The workshops invite participants into these ideas and practices. Because she believes in the power of this work to transform lives, Chené also trains others to facilitate these workshops.

Chené was born and raised by the ocean in Port Elizabeth, South Africa. She completed her doctoral degree in Practical Theology, specialising in pastoral therapy at the University of South Africa in 2006. She now resides in Pretoria.

To learn how to bring Transformation's workshops, coaching and consulting to your location, visit our website at www.transformations.co.za. You can reach Chené at chene@transformations.co.za.

THE VOICES OF THE READERS

"In her ground breaking work, using the lens of the Narrative process, Chené Swart opens the eyes of our souls to the importance of the stories by which we live and by which we are either imprisoned or liberated. As a group of US Catholic Sisters, we found ourselves in awe of what Chené and the Narrative process evoked in us in terms of understanding and articulating the story we ARE living, and its importance for our world and planet. We are humbled and delighted to be a part of *Re-Authoring the World: The Narrative Lens and Practices for Organisations, Communities and Individuals*."

> — *Nancy Conway,* CSJ, Ph.D. member of the leadership team,
> The Congregation of St. Joseph, USA

"What a gift Chené has brought to the world, with the book *Re-authoring the World: The Narrative Lens and Practices for Organisations, Communities and Individuals*! This is a handbook for anyone wishing to construct a different kind of living – a living of their own choosing and design. This book challenges us to deeply reflect on and put to one side those aspects of our lives which we have either consciously or unconsciously authorised others to create for us. This book lets us know that we have permission to re-author our lives. This wonderful handbook provides us with the tools of the Narrative practice which enable us to re-author and begin the journey of re-creating our lives. Thanks, Chené!"

> — *Olivia Saunders*, professor at The College/University of The Bahamas, a voice of the
> potential and possibility for an economy that serves all people,
> their communities and the world

"This book shows a new way to reconcile – based on local, cultural practices – business strategies with respect for the human work communities that constitute our organisations. More and more, coaches, organisational development consultants and leaders are interested in working with these ideas. This is the very first reference work about Narrative coaching and organisational practices by the most gifted practitioner and teacher of her generation."

> — *Pierre Blanc-Sahnoun*, MBA, Narrative coach and therapist,
> founding member of EMCC-France and author of *The Art of Coaching*

"Chené encourages us all to re-tell ourselves into being, because indeed words do open up worlds. Her work marks a moment in the West's seemingly endless expansion, where it can begin to grapple with its legacy of destruction in order to reweave humanness into the world's future. We need a world where the dominant story is one of the sustainability of life, relationships, and also the love that sustains us across time."

> — *Sayra Pinto* M.F.A , consultant, poet and author of *Pinol: Poems* and *Vatolandia*. Senior
> Fellow at the Suffolk University Center for Restorative Justice, Boston, Massachusetts

"This book is a gift for our times ... for all of us working to support change in the world at this particular moment in our great 'evolutionary story'. Especially for those of us schooled in organisational development, Chené has brought fresh light to the conversation. By taking Narrative Therapy from an individual to a collective and cultural level, she has allowed us to enter that possibility. Power and power relationships are framed and understood in new, life-affirming ways. 'Words [do indeed] open worlds' ... and the words of this book open up current ways of doing and being."

> — *Deborah Prokipchuk Ackley*, Organisation Development consultant and poet

"The narrative a community accepts as their story can shape who they become. Negative patterns are not easy to change. Chené, in this remarkable book, explains how we can build a new narrative for ourselves, our children and our neighbours, in turn choosing the future we want. I highly recommend this book to anyone who is interested in how communities can change."

> — *Paul Born*, President of and coach at the Tamarack Institute for Community
> Engagement and bestselling author of *Community Conversations*

"Chené's work strikes a new chord in the continuing effort of people everywhere to fashion lives of authentic expression. It does that by urging us to make use of the revolutionary power of naming our worlds. *Re-Authoring the World* invites us to look afresh at questions of which phenomena ought to be spoken about and who ought to do the speaking. When we bring forward those stories which matter to us and tell them in our own voices, argues Chené, we transform ourselves and social relations in our communities, and we build the power to dismantle those social structures established to render some people 'disposable'. Act on Chené's invitation and become part of transforming our world."

— *Tracey Thompson*, Director and oral historian "From Dat Time":
Oral and Public History Institute, University of The Bahamas

"Chené has gifted the coaching and consulting community with a Narrative Practice field book that simply makes sense. The practices she so deftly names and illustrates come up alongside the vast toolkit of our field and take their rightful place among the most useful few. If you aren't prepared to have a different relationship to problem-saturated stories and live into a new narrative or help people, teams, organisations or communities to do so, read it for the inspirational stories of mothers and 'leaders', managers and miners, neighbourhoods and nations who are doing the essential work of re-authoring the world."

— *Lisa Connors*, hybrid consultant, NeXtwork Partners, Detroit, USA

"Chené's *Re-Authoring the World* is a lucid, in-depth perspective for everyone who is interested in the transformative art of collaboration. Narrative techniques and approaches will be key for unlocking collective wisdom. Her work will inform, instruct and invite practices for creating together a world worthy of our best selves."

— *Alan Briskin*, Ph.D., co-author, *The Power of Collective Wisdom* and author of,
The Stirring of Soul in the Workplace

"There have been pioneers who have bridged disciplines to bring wisdom from a body of knowledge that had not yet been brought into the field of organisational development. Peter Senge did it with systems thinking and David Kantor took insights from family therapy to explain how coaches can read a team's communications dynamics. Chené Swart has unlocked the wisdom of Michael White and David Epston's years of work with Narrative Therapy and brought it to the fields of coaching and organisational development. Chené has applied her deep understanding of the most profound aims of Narrative Therapy – to honour the story we each hold within us as a unique and unfolding identity to be cherished – to guiding people through a transformative process. This is her gift to the world. This book delivers that gift."

— *Christine Cavanaugh-Simmons*, consultant, coach and author of
The Three Stories Leaders Tell: The What and Way of Using Stories to Lead

"Many books offer ways for us to improve the world. However, in skimming the surface with 'tips' and 'tools', few succeed in offering direction for the transformative change we need now more than ever. In *Re-authoring the World*, Chené Swart offers us a courageous approach that reaches deep into the fabric of our shared realities – the stories we tell about 'the way things are'. She gifts us with a practice which is central to a resilient future for humanity: the ability to edit and re-tell the stories that shape the foundation of our communities and organisations. The purpose? To engage together in real and practical ways of creating more spacious possibilities for our common futures."

— *Alexander Fink*, social work and youth work practitioner and instructor in Leadership
Education and Development at the University of Minnesota-Twin Cities

"In this book, Chené offers up the powerful work of Narrative practice with a simplicity and authenticity that demonstrate the essence of the work itself – developing and maintaining, as leaders and members of any community, a relentless commitment to curiosity, inquiry and the exploration of alternative perspectives. Chené's work, and the powerfully present manner in which she delivers it, have gifted our organisation with a greater sense of awareness and attention to the stories we tell – the powerful ways in which they shape our shared experiences, frame our relationships, and impact our success – and ultimately the power we hold, personally and collectively, to re-narrate them."

— *Sheelagh Davis*, coordinator of Learning & Development,
BC Nurses' Union, British Columbia, Canada

"This book will 'make a mark' in Narrative practice. *Re-authoring the World* will do what Peter Senge's *Field Book* did for organisational learning, offering Narrative practitioners an accessible 'how to' book grounded in theory, yet geared to practice. Chené's starting point and framework are simple, yet robust: *if you don't like the story you're in, then change the story. Re-authoring the World* goes on to offer practice-based perspectives on *how to* change the story – how to confront our taken-for-granted beliefs, identify a preferred narrative, and re-author our stories when we become stuck in narratives that no longer serve us. That's Chené's gift to us – a narrative toolbox for changing our selves by changing our stories."

— *Nick Nissley*, ED.D Dean of Business Technologies,
Cincinnati State Technical and Community College, Cincinnati, USA

"This book is an extremely valuable and needed contribution to the field of Narrative. It is a must-read for experienced and aspiring Narrative practitioners alike, as well as anyone seeking to affect transformation in human systems. The practices in this book, consistently applied, have the potential to bring about lasting transformative change in individuals, families, communities, organisations, countries and, as the title suggests, maybe even the world."

— *Sonja Blignaut*, Narrative practitioner, coach and founder of More Beyond Pty Ltd.

"This book represents a refreshing departure from the current trend to produce purely how-to-do-it therapy manuals. It captures the spirit of Narrative work, where the personal becomes political. Never fear, though, it also becomes the definitive word on how to apply Narrative ideas to the area of coaching and consulting."

— *Jeffrey Zimmerman*, Ph.D, Director of Bay Area Family Therapy Training Associates;
author of *If Problems Talked: Narrative Therapy in Action*

"This book is a must-read for organisation development practitioners who want to deepen their effectiveness with clients. In *Re-Authoring the World*, Chené Swart takes us beyond the *methodologies* of change to the use of a Narrative lens as a philosophical foundation. From this stance, the skills, gifts and knowledge held by the client are used to guide the work and the consultant becomes a co-journeyer in the choosing and thickening of a preferred narrative. Whether you are coaching individuals or working with a large organisation, this book will give you skills to help your clients experience enduring transformation!"

— *Gayle Hilleke*, MSOD, AU/NTL Class 39, Narrative Organisation Development practitioner

"This book is not just about discovering the transformational nature within Narrative practices, but is also about the beauty and abundance within, around and between us. It is a compendium of ways of thinking and conversing in a postmodern Narrative paradigm that will serve various generations of consultants, parents, psychologists, counsellors, life coaches, leaders, educators, clergymen, etc. Chené uses her own narrative and weaves it together with other voices, forming a 'continuous-in-the-making quilt' that gives warmth, depth and a multitude of possibilities. She embraces diversity and deconstructs power themes with respect and grace. Herewith my appreciation and thanks to Chené for sharing her journey and thoughts unreservedly."

— *Carl S du Preez*, Educational Psychologist, Narrative Practitioner, research coach,
nature lover and Director of the Network for Life Centre

"More often than not, chronic, lifestyle-related diseases are at least partially the result of a number of unsound health choices patients have made repetitively over time. Healing requires such patients to recognise their harmful health habits and the stories sustaining these, and to develop alternative health stories that will enable them to start living towards a different health outcome. Healthcare practitioners can play a vital role as facilitators in this process, though this is often easier said than done. This book has inspired me to listen more deeply and widely, and given me a new perspective on living my role as facilitator to patients committed – or committing – to developing their alternative health stories."

— *Dr Sarah le Grange*, phytotherapist

"The Narrative approach laid out in this brilliant book will provide you with insights, new frameworks and tools, but, more importantly, a strong sense of agency. Through our multiplicity of stories we connect and see one another as human becomings. Having people like Chené Swart in this world is a gift and a blessing for any community. Thank you!"

— *Tue Juelsbo*, Kaospilot and management consultant

"*Re-Authoring the World* will change the way you perceive yourself and your place in the world. It's been said that you see the world as you are, and the self-knowledge you gain as a reader of the book, will give you the tools which are required to make the internal shifts necessary in re-authoring your perception of not only yourself, but many of the taken-for-granted assumptions and perceived limitations that have shaped your understanding of the world. Chené Swart possesses the gift of passion for transformation on the personal, social, spiritual and emotional levels of life. Her expertise as a deep listener in her workshops has provided the public with the gift of various nuanced observations about the human experience, and this will offer readers the tools and approaches they need to radically transform their lives and the lives of others around them."

— *Siyade Gemechisa*, M.S., producer for Sandscribe Media,
social activist and co-creator of a re-authored world

"Chené Swart's new book will take your breath away. I am overcome by the power of the narrative. It is not just about the individual story but the power of the collective story for our families, communities, organisations and nations ... This is a must-read for a world seeking hope and change."

— *Joan O. Wright*, MSW, MCC, leadership and organisational development consultant.
Author of *UP: Pursuing Significance in Leadership and Life*

"*Re-Authoring the World* is a powerful, important and heartfelt book that reminds us again and again to consciously take ownership of the stories we tell about our world and ourselves. Further, it offers us profoundly elegant tools and practices that support us in re-authoring the stories that reside at the core of our identity."

— *Gary Petersen*, Principal of Petersen and Associates, and
Director of Public Works for the City of Salinas, California

"Through her inspiring story and the power of Narrative frameworks, Chené invites us to consciously discover and choose the best of who we are and who we are becoming. *Re-Authoring the World* offers an insightful and activating lens for leadership and personal development."

— *Valerie Nishi*, BSc, MBA, leadership development educator, The Refinery Leadership
Partners and co-founder of the Women's Leadership Foundation

"I was struck by the power of this Narrative practice and Chené's ability to describe it in a way that is practical and very helpful to me, as an individual and as a coach. The gifts I received from this book were the gift of her voice and her eloquence in sharing her knowledge and insights, as well as the gift of a new approach and questions I can use to promote deeper insights, understandings and transformation."

— *Gail Angelo*, Managing Principal of a firm focused on executive coaching and leadership

"Chené Swart is masterful in using the techniques of Narrative Therapy in groups, in order to have conversations that can transform our lives, communities and world. This book gives me great hope that we can change our problem stories and create the alternative communities we desire. If you are a person who longs for transformation in our families, cities and communities, this is the book for you."

— *Marie Hogan*, CSJ social worker and member of the Congregation of St. Joseph

"*Re-Authoring the World* unveiled a basket of gifts, as it took me on a journey through Narrative work. By reflecting on each chapter, my understanding of this body of knowledge is continually influenced and enriched. There are so many stories that are ready to be re-authored and lives to be transformed. This book presents readers with a tremendous amount of insights and examples to uncover and explore an alternative world of possibilities."

— *Gerhard Redelinghuys*, leadership development specialist, South Africa

"Chené's writing is refreshing and cleansing, liberating and daunting, like standing under an exotic waterfall! She highlights possibility, not problem, taking us to a place that questions our ingrained cultural and social beliefs and what we allow to define us. She shows us how to untangle ourselves from what are often stifling and homogenised ideas that are passed down from generation to generation, how to free ourselves of other people's notions and expectations of who they think we are or should be. Chené also shows us how the simple use of language, the words we choose, can affect how we see ourselves and relate to each other in such profound and reverberating ways. She clarifies the relationship between the individual and the collective, helping us to understand that how we view ourselves affects the whole world – past, present and future. She opens us up to realise how we've willingly become victims of our own self-constructed narratives that are so limiting, and she empowers us to rewrite and reconstruct. This realisation is both terrifying and beautiful because of the potential for change; it is only through this realisation that the shift to happiness and freedom can come to us, which then, in turn, has the possibility to transform into happiness and freedom on a global scale.

Chené's book has given me the gifts of understanding and hope, truth and transparency. It has opened me to see with clarity the gift of freedom I have as an artist, and how my own art can be a vehicle for change. I can create a world – paint an image from my perspective, from how I feel, choose the colours and create a window into newness, into possibility that can, in turn, open up newness and possibility for others. Beauty isn't in the image, it's in the individuality."

— *Danielle Acerra*, artist

"The gifts that I received were that the Narrative approach helps to get us un-stuck from being a victim of circumstances. I now understand how to reframe reality through re-authoring. The Narrative approach is an appreciative approach that focuses on possibility, not only on the problem."

— *Francois Steyn*, Managing Director of Gravitas Organisation Development Consultants

"*Re-authoring the World* is fiercely and wonderfully written. I have an image of an orchestra led by a beautiful conductor – Chené brings all the diverse instruments into harmony and symphony. Chené is that conductor, in a way, and 're-authoring' is just like conducting: giving voices back to those who thought they were voiceless and without talent."

— *Khulukazi Fungiwe Dlakavu*, Managing Member of Dlakavu Psychology Consulting

"Human beings are story-making creatures. In her wise and generous book, Chené Swart taps our deep instinct for story to fuel and enrich the ways we work and live together in these challenging times."

— *Barbara McAfee*, author of *Full Voice: The Art and Practice of Vocal Presence*

"Re-Authoring the World has a way with words that pulls the reader in close and as it celebrates the voice of personal experience, it invites a deeper consideration of subjectivity and what informs it. Chené's work reveals a loyalty to the ideas of Narrative Therapy and her passion for its creative capacity to engage transformation is persuasive."

— *Hilda Nanning*, MSW, RSW, RCC, Narrative Therapy educator and therapist

"Chené provides an insightful contribution to Narrative work that presents both the simplicity and complexity of this way of seeing the world, making it readable for interested parties across a broad spectrum."

— *Lyn Lupke*, psychologist

"This book is needed for a generation that is in a continual state of authorship through social media and never-ending connectivity. Our individual and collective stories must also be re-authored at an increasing speed, as culture and technology change at an ever-increasing speed."

– *Andy Sontag*, a KaosPilot

"Narrative approaches to learning, counselling, coaching and therapy signal a break with the traditional focus on pathology, and instead provide a powerful way in which to focus on growth and aspiration. Chené Swart has created practical ways in which this discipline is turned from concept and philosophy into practice and deeds. Her work already forms an important part of the Post-graduate Diploma in Leadership at the University of Stellenbosch Business School, and has influenced my own thinking and practice as a consultant, coach and facilitator of development programmes on MBA degrees. It deserves the widest possible recognition and will help enhance the capabilities of anyone who is involved or interested in aspirational personal growth."

– *Christo Nel*, Programme Director of Executive and International MBA Programmes; Assistant Professor Leadership at Nyenrode Business University in the Netherlands and author of *Transformation without Sacrifice*

This incredibly empowering book is a must-read for anyone looking for the strength, courage and determination to share in the transformation of our world. Be prepared to shift your attitude, to be inspired, and to grow and expand in all ways thinkable! "

– *Annalise Jennings*, Director of Dynamic Exchange, author and creator of 'Whole of Community Change' Transforming Indigenous communities ... one narrative at a time!

"In *Re-authoring the World*, Chené Swart gives us the inspiration and the tools to shift our thinking and change our future. By sharing her own story – and the stories of individuals and groups around the world – she gives us the ability to see through a new lens and use a new language to reshape our own narratives and those of our neighbourhoods and communities. What a gift!"

– *Leslie Stephen*, editor, www.abundantcommunity.com

INDEX

[Created with **TExtract**/ www.Texyz.com]